DIARY OF FIRE

GW00601021

DIARY OF FIRE

BY

Igino Giordani

New City London

First published under the title *Diario di fuoco*
by Città Nuova, Roma

First published in Great Britain 1981
by Mariapolis Ltd.
57 Twyford Avenue, London W3 9PZ

© 1981 New City London

Printed in Great Britain by
Biddles Ltd, Guildford, Surrey

ISBN 0 904287 17 3

CONTENTS

Foreword   vii

1941   1
1942   8
1943   13
1944   17
1945   21
1946   23
1947   25
1948   31
1949   41
1951   43
1954   43
1956   48
1957   51
1958   56
1959   65
1960   68
1961   91
1963   92
1964   103
1965   112
1966   114
1968   114

FOREWORD

A diary, especially if it is a spiritual one, assumes a place all its own, one of pre-eminence, and rightly so, in auto-biographical literature. Very often, in fact, written without literary pretensions and without any thought of publication, it serves the author as a means of fixing states of mind, confessions, resolutions and interior advances with absolute sincerity. As if the expression in writing of ideas and feelings strengthened their intensity and contributed to ensuring their permanence within the person.

A document of this sort is then precious, since it allows the reader to acquaint himself more easily with the author's interior world and so to ascertain better the driving forces which have inspired the whole of his work, to discover the various influences he has under-gone, to establish his kinship with and his divergence from contemporary writers and finally, to communicate with him fully and surely in view of a deeper under-standing of his witness and his dedication.

The publication of these pages by Igino Giordani is justified by these principles. Although short, considering the lengthy period over which they extend, they afford nonetheless a portrait of a cultured man wholly taken up, as a result of his faith, in the Christian 'adventure' (an expression very dear to him) and in contact with the whole range of contemporary problems, constantly resolved by him with a steadfast loyalty to the highest and most authentic ideals: "One thing alone matters, and this absolutely: Jesus Christ", is his opening sentence.

An authentic man then, because an authentic Christian. A thirst for the Absolute, penetrated by the tensions belonging to his state of life and gradually purified by the vision of his own humanity, his own ineffective impulses – "I do not accomplish the good which I desire . . ." as St. Paul writes to the Romans – which in time were calmed by a vision, ever more enlightened and experiential, of his relationship with God and of the mediatory and exemplary role of Mary.

As the burden of years came to make itself felt, the trenchant power of the apologist, a characteristic of Giordani that was universally recognised and so ingrained in him that it stands out undiminished even in so personal a work as the present, is accompanied by a more sedate vigour, affecting his inmost being, in an increasing closeness to the Eternal.

His awareness of being consecrated is also remarkable: a consecration lived as a layman in the setting of the Focolare Movement, and recalling the assertion of the Fathers of the Church which appears very frequently in his speeches: a married man must live like a monk, minus celibacy. Written without embellishments, the author at times pokes fun even at himself in terms which may cause some astonishment but which are evidence of the freedom he had attained, this "Diary of Fire" seems to become the symbol and standard of the "difficulties of the Christian today" (the title of one of his books) and of the yearning for the Absolute which runs through the generation in which we are living, in spite of the disintegrating and materialistic forces that are at work.

1941

May – One thing alone matters, and this absolutely: Jesus Christ.

All the rest has only a relative importance.

Relative to him, it goes without saying.

You worry about so many events and people around you, in order to put your own little self in the centre of things – a wobbly hinge and one that will not stand up to any strain. Put God in the centre and he will be like a monolith in the midst of a cloud of midges. He will not be disturbed and there will be no more disturbances in you. Would you have God concern himself with revolutions and persecutions, conflicts and aggressions? It only takes him a puff of breath to disperse them into the nothing from which envy brought them forth.

Why be so disquieted if the world harasses you on account of your faith? That harassing of you by the world is the confession which the world gives to Christ on your behalf and to you on Christ's behalf. The world disquiets you because God is in you: and if God is in you, you possess peace in its totality. And peace is the fruit of conscience and strength.

Difficulties arise in social life when selfishness and hatred enter in. Love on the other hand dissipates them. If your heart is tormented by scruples, let go of it from the top of the slope of God's love; think of what Christ would have done in your place and do the same as far as you can.

The dogmas of the Trinity, the Incarnation and the Immaculate Conception emerge from their abstruse and dark fixedness if love illuminates it; then they become family secrets. They are facts of love and love presses its suit on God: it is God who lives and acts, who understands and rejoices.

And everything in religion is first and foremost love.

The soul that is invaded by the love of God radiates. Even the eyes of the body, though they may be in sick orbits as those of Paul were, shine like the pupils of small children that overflow with happiness from the depths of their innocence.

The soul which loves is not harassed by suspicions: it trusts in its guardian angel and is not afraid of evil because it sees only good, and it knows well that with the Supreme Good there is no need for fears.

Love is the soul of God in us. It rises above the dimensions of our body and of our life and tends to expand to infinity, because the soul of God is infinite. It is anti–limit, anti–division, anti–differentiation. Cosmic and hyper–cosmic, it makes the universe its own, as the child of its own expansion.

To be so taken up with serving the Lord as to have no time for sanctifying oneself! (Apparently, for, in fact, this *is* sanctification).

The Lord is served also in one's brethren, his creatures. Since they are his likeness, you see the Lord visibly in them and you love him in each one of them.

And to serve is to love in deeds.

Man is a social animal. In the sphere of the Absolute his society is the Church. But it is not to be supposed that the more persons you rub shoulders with, the more Christian social life is achieved. The Communion of Saints is not a political meeting. Neither is it a gossip shop. It is brought about in the spirit and not in worldly contacts. It is in proportion not to the number of Christians you rub shoulders with but to the services that you render and to the value of the souls with which you unite yourself in Christ to form his Body.

Separating oneself from the world does not mean separating oneself from men. The world is in the likeness

2

of Satan: men are in the likeness of Christ, your brothers, redeemed by the one Blood. To separate yourself from them is equivalent to denying your kinship with them in God, substituting for the worship of the common Father and Redeemer the unrestrained adoration of your own self.

One can be separated from the world and yet live in Wall Street: one can be separated from one's brothers while being shareholders in a company with a thousand members. The hermit is not cut off from the Communion of Saints; he is offered for his brethren; he lives by dying for them.

The more your soul is inserted into the Mystical Body, the more of Christ's life it absorbs and the more it must communicate of Christ's life, to others; a branch that transmits the sap, not one that blocks its flow; for that would be the same as being cut off. Cut off from your brothers, cut off from Christ.

How easy it is to act the part of someone important, or a superior person, when one is seated in the highest and most comfortable stalls of the social assembly! And how easy it is to pose as a sage when one enjoys a bountiful income, combined with health, power and honours. But it is difficult to keep your spirits up and maintain the role of a sage when one is living through the sombre experience of misery, slander and ingratitude: when one is suffering temptation.

> Humility and charity;
> serving all,
> feeling oneself inferior to all,
> because the mark of God is upon all,
> Christ died for all.
> Pride alone makes you lonely and sad.

What a responsibility! Trying to be a Christian writer that is, an Apostle – without being holy!

3

When one is full of oneself there is no room for God.

2 May – Lord, in my day this is the hour of the rending of my 'ecclesial' flesh, in that portion where my person is bound to the body of the Church. At this hour the Enemy lacerates my flesh from outside and from inside, in the place where this flesh comes to birth, in the family, flesh of my flesh, which becomes 'the Church'. It is the great trial, in which everything seems to fall to pieces, in mockery. But I have abandoned myself to you, and whatever may happen, you do not abandon me.

If you serve God to please men – even though they are men consecrated to God – you are on the wrong path. Such a service usually brings with it troubles on earth. And this incomprehension also is bitter water that forms part of the trial.

And realise that, as far as most people are concerned, you will not be judged by your true interior worth but by what you appear to be outwardly. It is not your virtues, your dedication, or your work that will be put to your credit; but the kind of car you use and the titles and decorations that lend weight to your clothes and to your visiting card. Therefore do not grow proud if people praise you for what you are outwardly, and do not think the worse of yourself if people do not recognise you for what you do and are inwardly – in the realm of the spirit. If you attend to the true and the good, you risk ostracism; something which will make even your friends, who will judge you with the judgment of the powerful and the rich, leave you in total isolation. Then you can remain alone like Christ in the Garden. It is a grace which he will accord you.

Enhance your writings by your life.
Enhance your life by your writings.

The vanity of all means, etymologically, that all is empty. An immense emptiness, made to be filled up with God.

Regrets, disappointments, upsets, interior conflicts, come from this: that you say you are working for the Church and then see only yourself: yourself, a miserable obstruction blocking the light. But you must disappear to make room for Christ: so that Christ may live in you and no longer yourself. You will be all when you are with Christ, identified with him, otherwise you remain a nonentity.

The man who humiliates me, reinvigorates me. The man who offends me, strengthens me. My slanderer is my friend; my enemy is my benefactor. Men abandon us in order that we may be left alone, just God and I.

Love is a gift and it is given gratuitously. It gives itself and abandons itself without any thought of receiving a return. You must love as God loves without the possibility of recompense. Be prepared rather for incomprehension and treachery. For love can be mistaken for weakness and love can be thought to confer a right to receive from the giver, with the result that the one benefited can look upon himself as a benefactor. And in a sense this is true: when love brings pain, then, if this is allowed to mingle with the cup of the Precious Blood, it becomes the inebriating wine of your happiness.

Besides, if you wish to be crucified with Christ (and you do wish for this) the only course open to you is to go up on to Calvary: the Cross is at the end of the *Via Dolorosa*.

Holiness goes unnoticed by most people. An insignificant woman, an unremarkable man, passes by and that is all you see: you see people who do not wish to attract attention. Holiness is noticed by saints and it is noticed by intellectuals. As with Jesus in Galilee, where he was identified by the disciples who loved him most ardently and therefore attached themselves to him and by demoniacs, men possessed by the Enemy, who therefore begged him to depart from them. The great sinner, the pervert, the heretic, have an instinctive awareness of holiness: they abominate it and keep it at a distance.

Take a look at the wearisome and costly trappings – clothes, trinkets and attitudes – with which other people, just like yourself, endeavour to give themselves a personality: to cover up an empty expanse of window with expensive rags. And consider the sentimentality, the affected looks and smiles with which they try to snare one another, bird-catchers that are caught in their own snares. But the moment you look on the other side of the covering, you find that it is nothing but a cushion put over an emptiness. . . . There is a void within you and a void within them. And if you do not fill it with God, nothing is left you but to despair. It is he who puts reality into appearances, totality into nothingness. And when you have understood this, it's as when sun and wind have scattered fantastic wreathings of mist and lay bare vistas of strength and joy.

What a mob this is, held together by chatteration and by the fumes of perspiration and scent. You are in the midst of it and you are alone. At your side you have men and women, religious people dedicated to the service of their neighbour, and you are alone. You are in a tide of humanity and it is as if you were in a desert. Nonetheless, start to live in the Church, with the Church, that is, have yourself enrolled in the fellowship of the saints, in which Christ is, and all these strangers become members of your own body, spirit of your spirit. They are poor creatures who try to get along by out-worn childish tricks; but they are members of Christ and therefore they are a part of Christ: they are such that through them Christ communicates himself to us and we communicate ourselves to him. Recipients of the sacraments, they are vehicles of sanctity, warp and woof of the Church. The Word becomes flesh mystically in them: and their life becomes your life also.

November – Disappointments and sacrifices are neither disappointments nor sacrifices: they are means for re-discovering the reality of relationship: God and you. Disappointments and sacrifices empty out human material in order that the divine spirit may penetrate into the space left free. Men leave you in order that God may take you back.

If you were to find more time for talking with the Blessed Virgin you would acquire entirely fresh resources for dealing with God and with men, for knowledge and for life. The contact alone would purify you more than all your studies and endeavours can do.

People given to activity spend and spread: they spend chiefly words, they spread chiefly ink. They shout and they give battle, but their strength is obtained, to a great extent, from the store into which there filters, in silence, from the shadows, the holiness of souls who look more at God than at the earth, or who look at men only in God and for him. Mysticism is the soul of action.

What the Christ of the Eucharist makes us experience is not desire: it is hunger.

I cannot think of my mother without rising again to the thought of Christ's mother, because her destiny as a working-class woman, one who lived in suffering and want, in unremitting toil, recalls to me the image of that Israelite maiden, pierced by seven swords. She was still alive – before she died amidst the torments of a surgical operation better described as a butchery – and already the thought of her and the image of her brought me more anguish than tenderness, because that stern face, the face of an Etruscan woman, bore marks and reminders of suffering, her own and that of her kinsfolk, that of a whole tragic generation. Her smile issued from the threshold of a spasm of pain, she smiled for us, but she was suffering, mourning and praying within herself. Not given to displays of feeling, she rarely kissed her children, except when they were going away or when they were returning from long absences; but in her reserve, she lived for them and wore herself out for them; she devoured them with her eyes; she waited up for them at night, saying rosaries, and then, at their return, she made it her business to fortify their spirit, in order to sow in it, all unlettered as she was, the seeds of the knowledge of God. She was drained of blood when she died: and it was an offering to Christ, from whom she had drawn all her sustenance.

1942

1 February – A little silence. . . . *Hearing* silence, and within its dark bosom hearing again the melody of the stars, with the echo of the purest melodies of men: the voices, soft and loud, of the house and of my brothers . . .; and further back, in the recollected dark, the silent decomposition of my cells: feeling my own dying within life, and at the same time the very formation of the soul, atom by atom, to eternal life within present death, like the patient preparation of a chrysalis within the blood-bespattered shell, to emerge in freedom.

17 March – There is a plaster-cast Saint that is a caricature, a complete reversal of the truth: a dumb creature, lacking eyes to see, ears to hear and heart to burn: he neither sees nor hears nor utters; aloof from passion, because mutilated by life; in the midst of men yet absent, withdrawn and frozen, like a fossil ruminating, without a spark of affection for his brothers, on the pretext of loving the Lord alone. Glacial, he has no commitments, does not contract responsibilities; does not interefere and does not formulate opinions; his principal virtue lies in perfect neutrality. He is considered to be a saint because he is abject; wise because ambiguous; virtuous because stupid; he is considered in a word to be an angel because he is a goose.

12 May – If you write and speak about God and religion the first fruit is yours; those words commit you before your conscience, before men and before God; and, unless you are an impostor, no other course is left open to you but to become a saint. Only a saint can speak about religion; simply by speaking about religion you can perhaps become a saint; because only thus do those reiterated words commit your soul.

An immense benefit of union with God is, meanwhile, this: that you are free from the man who is a slave. From the man who is a slave, and from his stupidity; from his hatred and from his perfidy. Even if he sows death around you, defames you and drives you out from his haunts and from his pleasures, you – with God – are free; and in the end, you understand that there is no other satisfaction in living but preserving your freedom, bought for you with the Blood of Christ, by keeping yourself free from sin, that principal impediment to union with God. This then gives you strength to love and serve even the man who is a slave.

Religion gradually isolates you from a large number of people. It acts upon you as if you were walking away from a square resounding with strident noises; gradually they grow faint, die away and are heard no more. But you do not remain alone: for all the empty souls that you lose, you find as many pure souls, full of God; and a whole new city – the City of God – is revealed to your soul; and a new network of affections binds you to a new community of citizens – the citizens of the City of God. You pass out of the noisy square and enter the silent church: into the communion of saints, where you attain communion with God.

But this is the way of it – always so. I rejoice in the world, with the world, according to the flesh; and I lose the sight of God and of the spirit. Suffering returns, and, like a North wind, sweeps away fumes and dust and uncovers once again the fatherly light of God, and this suffering becomes the vehicle of a joy made of love alone.

If you look at men, at once you are moved to make comparisons; and from these will come envy; and from envy gossip; in a word you fall on to the stony ground of petty things.

But if you lift your gaze to Christ Crucified, he at once draws you to himself, to his arms, stretched out in a straight line and wide open to the infinite: from that height the differences between men disappear and the whole mass of them appears to you only as the hillock on which the Cross is planted and on to which his Blood rains.

17 June – Religious life moves forward as long as it tends to God, with the power of God; otherwise it does not move at all, it becomes clogged. Human forces give a first impetus, one however which is no more than human: the great space of the divine is traversed only by catching hold of God. When you lean upon a man, even if he be a saint, you find that at a certain moment the support gives way. It gives way because what is human cannot replace the divine. A man, whoever he may be, can offer you a springboard, he cannot be a summit. To fly we need wings and wings are fashioned

10

in the Absolute. Let it not be said, at the moment when his strength fails, that a man – even a saint – has deceived us. He could not give what he did not possess. He could teach you the road: but it is you who must travel the road, with the power that God alone gives you.

To love is to serve.
Draw the consequences.

November – It is very difficult to enter deeply into the realm of mystery, if suffering, like an explosive charge, does not first shatter into fragments the thick rind, the stony layer of selfishness. The blows which nature and men deliver are, finally, levelled against that covering, and open a road marked out with sharp-edged debris, the impact of which tears the flesh.

Religious life is menaced by a parasite, which, to give it an historical name, could be called pharisaism; that is a sticky superstratum of worldly conventions, very earthly interests, a formalism that is alien to the spirituality and simplicity of true religion: and it forms a coating which, gradually growing colder in virtue of its own intrinsic frigidity, becomes a hard crust, within which charity gasps for breath, faith vacillates and hope swells into arrogance.

20 November – If you listen to the radio what you hear is, in one way or another, talk of sinkings, air raids, carnage and plans for continuing all this. If you read the newspaper, it is, as it has been for years, a tragic and haunting tale of slaughter, famine, fires, death and blood. And if we listen to ourselves, it is not so much the suffering and the hunger from which we suffer that assails us as the thought that the next man does not suffer more; in our spasms of pain we think of how we may bring about more suffering. It is a moral reversal to which we are abandoned: people who wish to build from the top downwards, walk on their heads, turn universal gravitation upside down. We are born for life, and we work for death; and whereas love alone resolves difficulties, we have built up our whole system of ideas on a foundation of hate. As if we had been put into the world for nothing else but to make our stay intolerable. All this is a sign that the place where we shall have peace is not here.

25 November – Bitterness, illness, renunciations. . . . This is life: a preparation for death.

The death that wounds most deeply is not only that which robs us of the persons dear to us; but also that which kills feelings of affection: the death that takes place within us and rends us.

This is the test: not allowing the passions to get the better of one, beginning with despair: not being subject to fits of anger, bitterness, disappointment: one must master them, burn them out as one would a viper's nest, in the fire of God's love.

19 December – Nations spend on arms and wars two thirds of their wealth, the best of their manpower, a large part of their science, time and dignity. Beneath the fiery light of Satan, murder has become the most essential occupation. A proof that, where God has been driven out, stupidity enters in.

A superficial judgement calls love weakness. And instead it is hatred that is weakness. Love is a disposition which gives and therefore draws on existent powers; hatred tends to withdraw power from others, and so it confesses its own weakness. Hatred is what alcohol is to the organism: it gives a momentary energy but leaves behind a greater physical prostration.

27 December – The dead who cause us the greatest suffering are those who die in our heart; for the heart, turned into a tomb, feels itself decaying with them.

Do not spoil the benefits of suffering by reactions of anger or by the inertia of despair. Overcome suffering with love.

These wars, with their convulsions and carnage and ruins, behind which groan the tortured spirits of innocent people are an explosion of Satan, who is the Murderer; and he feeds upon dead things; but they are also the revelation of a truth which the verbosity of wiseacres had obscured, namely that science, wealth, mechanisation and culture do not bring happiness and do not lead to progress. Science has given us more murderous explosives, culture has elaborated myths and theories for more savage fratricide. It is plain to see then that even with the internal combustion engine, radio and all the rest, the only possible human happiness consists in morality, warmed by charity.

Love resolves all; it heals all wounds, compensates for all harm done and sets free from all forms of servitude.

Take love away from life and life grows chilled. Take love out of social relationships and the whole earth becomes a North Pole. It is the lack of charity which has made of human life the most difficult of professions, that of the tragic actor.

1943

To feed oneself on pride or to nourish other people with pride is the same as to resort to alcohol as a tonic; one ends up drunk and incapacitated.

We must have the pride of Christ. To suffer our humiliations with fortitude, but to glorify Christ; to

13

check our feelings of anguish, and to exhibit the joy of Christ; to rise above our personal and family concerns, in order to care for Christ. So many humiliations, agonies and cares, on the human level, are only a blaze of dry grass; and all that remains, apart from a little black dust, is Christ.

Be praised, my Lord, who seasons my day with bitter herbs. They purify me, while earthly joys overwhelm me with the carnal exhalations of my own ego – clutter me up with vanities, a void crammed with vapours – turning me away from you. Only give me strength: for without your strength I collapse.

It is a very poor thing, the virtue which is mine in hours of ease, if it collapses easily in hours of difficulty, if it does not acquire such an autonomy that it will not fail in trials, violent and sudden attacks, changes on the part of others, irritating disappointments. It is virtue, that is it has a virile consistency, if it is not dependent on the humours of third persons, but depends solely on God, the Unchangeable, withstanding therefore the fury of the storm like granite.

1 March – All will go well, in the order of the divine good, when you will squeeze compassion for others out of all your suffering. Take antipathies, scorn, misunderstandings and give gentleness, charity and goodness. This is the chemical change which love brings about: the transubstantiation of charity.

18 April – Apostasy from revealed religion is not a return to natural religion: it is not a descent from the level of the supernatural to that of nature; but it is a leap from heaven to hell, like that of Lucifer, it is an engulfing in the Satanic. In fact there are no more perverse people than the apostates from Christianity. It is a good thing for them that Christ has pity even on their impiety.

28 April – Common Christian wisdom tells us that sin is born of pride; and this is manifestly and vigorously punished by God. In our times man had come to believe himself a superman; the biped described himself as God; theology was no longer of any use to him, he rejected the Church and denied God; science was enough for him; one or two declared themselves in public to be infallible; many others told themselves the same in private. Amidst the variety of non-Christian philosophy a Satanic pride had arisen: and now God is making use of their theories and scientific inventions to rain upon their heads a storm of explosives, crushing the edifice of their pride as a cyclone does a cardboard hut.

13 May – To describe peoples as being young or old has sense only if we mean by these terms the deterioration produced by sin and the rejuvenation which virtue brings about. We are worm-eaten by sin: this is the fact.

In the end, what counts is one thing alone: to become saints. The moment this ideal is relinquished, the descent is begun.

27 May – What is a saint? A Christian with a backbone.

21 June – If the test comes, my mind is ready: my heart too will be ready, if God helps it. May the hour of trial be the hour of grace. May the Lord grant that his worthless servant may not bear witness to him unworthily.

10 September – People are growing accustomed to living amidst death and hunger, amidst shame and lies: while I write the windows are shaking from gunfire; at night the sirens gather us into the shelters, and the shades of those who have been killed plead for our pity. If we understood that this is our passion – our contribution to the completion of Christ's passion – we would not waste all this suffering.

15

14 September – Lord, I make a show of serving my neighbour. I say that it is a duty. In its origin it is such. But you enlighten me and I see that it is a pleasure. The first service that I can render you is to entwine myself around your Cross; if I do what you will, if I say what you tell me, then my service will become, for others too, a pleasure.

2 October – First prayer, next integrity and activity, therefore what God wills.

16 October – The tragedy that is unfolding beneath our eyes, within our souls and within our bodies, presents above all this fearful element: that, at the sight of the ruin which has come upon unarmed and innocent people, a man is driven to doubt God's justice and his very existence. But in fact, God is just and God does exist, because he has given us freedom and lets us exercise it to the full. A consequence of this full exercise of our freedom allowed to us by him, are the griefs which we are mourning, brought about by ourselves because we use that gift to rebel against the Giver, living according to a law which is not God's but Satan's. Yet in leaving us this freedom and permitting these trials, he treats us as sons that have come of age. No longer infants but old enough to have the light and power to extricate ourselves from trouble by our own efforts: something that is entirely possible, granted that light and strength are his.

24 November – Do not spoil your suffering with impatience: transform it into love by patience. Then the Father will change it into glory by omnipotence.

6 December – Christ is an instrument for the reception of suffering. He is born for this. Suffering is his life of redemption.

11 December – If God sends us joys, let us be grateful to him for making us feel his heart; if he sends us trials, let us be grateful to him just the same, for giving us a share in his suffering.

Stupidity finds its support principally in pride. Where you come up against pride, dig down and you will find stupidity.

1944

17 January – By yourself you cannot move two steps without falling. Unite youself to Christ: the two of you form a pair which will go quite a long way. You will reach God.

22 January – The commandment is to serve your neighbour: to this is attached absolutely no promise of return or recompense from the brethren served. The reward is given by God. If then you look for gratitude and repayment from men, you are altering the economy of the Gospel: and you are committing a sin of stupidity.

7 February – Do not believe that the profession of a Christian is easier today than twenty centuries ago; or that it is less dangerous. If you are a true follower of Christ the expressions of your faith may take on today forms different from those of the apostolic age, but they remain a risk as those were or more exact a beatitude equal to them, for Christ has guaranteed the beatitude of suffering for justice, for everyone and for all time: therefore for you also and for your day.

Work therefore, serenely, as if you had to live for a long time, without boredom, and you will serve the Church; but be ready, at any moment, to get up from your desk, lay down your pen and surrender your body to suffering and even to death, for the cause of justice. You would authenticate your words by action. And justice is Christ.

9 February – This war has reduced both social and spiritual life to the simplest expressions. The former is becoming cannibalism. The latter is being reduced to a relationship between man and God, without anything interposed. Others abandon you, money is short, illusions collapse, as these buildings do beneath a bomb from an aeroplane. You are reduced to abandoning yourself either to death or to God, who is Life. Abandoned to God, you are in the last ditch, from which neither hunger nor war, not even the Satanic agents of the Beast will dislodge you.

What a quantity of wisdom I put into writing: and what a quantity of silliness I put into my actions.

16 February – The war is rumbling over our heads. From one moment to the next we may be blown away. Very well: the Lord knows which is best for us: life or death. May his will be done. The thought that he will dispose everything for our greater good and that to him I have committed the persons of those dear to me with the whole of myself, gives me, in the midst of War, great peace. In this desert created by human bestiality, which has set everyone, powerless and alone, face to face with death, how close God has come! And how vividly Dante's witness comes home: "*En la sua voluntade è nostra pace*" (In his Will is our peace).

25 February – Since circumstances have condemned you to a life of misery, take more care to die a good death; and it will be the most effective revenge on the homicidal stupidity of a society governed by secular morality.

1 March – All this hatred, all this agitation of muscles and ideologies, to build they say – something definitive; all this war: what products of stupidity. All that is intelligent and positive is love and compassion. The rest, riches, self-conceit, fame, exitement are but dry grass on a roof.

7 March – Anger does to the edifices of the spirit what a hurricane does to the tents of a camp; what one of these air raids does to a residential block: in a few minutes it demolishes constructions that have cost time and labour. Christian wisdom is measured also by the ability to control anger. Anger, however, is holy if it is unleashed against the constructions of the Evil One.

9 March – I am constantly realising afresh that Providence thinks of me much more (indeed, very much more) than I think of it. I keep it present for a few moments in my day: It keeps me present all the day long.

Every first movement of pride is checked the moment you consider that all that you have and all that you give, brains, and work, prayer and charity, is God's gift.

20 March – It is still but dawn and already enemy planes are bombing Rome. And bread, coal, light, water are in short supply. The trial (two wars, revolutions, destruction) has lasted since you entered on life. It must be said that the Lord has some regard for you, as for all your contemporaries, if he judges you able to undergo your trial in these conditions. Satan is exerting the best of his powers: God is giving the best of his graces; and for the man who yields to him, he changes this outward war into an infinite inward peace.

1 April – What is important and decisive is that as long as you do not suffer material want, you should not fall face downwards under the avalanche of the hatreds that come hurtling like rocks from every direction. You must keep on your feet, mastering this fury and not letting yourself be submerged by it. But it will not be easy.

19

4 April – The times are difficult: they can only be lived heroically or basely: mediocrity is not allowed. Rather this itself is the expiation for the moral mediocrity of the past generations and of our days up to the present: for having made light of God's law.

But God has great regard for us if he has subjected us to this trial and believed us capable of undergoing it. Now, it is a question of showing ourselves deserving of the esteem that he accords us.

17 April – What are you afraid of, man of little faith? The Father is with you, you are in the hands of the Almighty. And what could happen to you without his giving you the strength to endure in the storm and the grace to turn it to your good?

5 May – These last years, or days have been given us that we may witness our physical disintegration and attend to our moral edification; that we may realise the flimsiness of the world's structures and turn our hearts to the City of God. Illnesses, bereavements, collapses, hunger . . . the birthpangs of the soul which is being born to eternity.

17 August – Faith resolves suffering into love. Everything is resolved in love, in Christianity, which is an unceasing production of love. The struggle for life is a struggle for and against love. The Christian struggle is a continual defensive action to prevent love being overpowered.

18 October – Every day that is born is, as they say, a drawing nearer to death. And instead it is a drawing nearer to life, a tiresome extricating of oneself from this prison of death.

29 October – However well prepared you may be by historical studies, the bitterest surprise for you, now, is this: that in your doing of good you are misunderstood by the good, that in defence of religion you find yourself at odds with religious people: in order that your good may be wholly between you and God, and no human praise or, worse, earthly reward, may be interposed.

1945

17 January – By myself I do not move a step; but you and I, Lord, go to the ends of the earth.

22 April – War, misery, indifference, hate, fears . . . it is all explained with Christ. Without him it has no sense, it is an abyss and it summons to death. With him it is not only explained but becomes bearable: the abyss no longer frightens: it may rob us even of our clothes, isolate us by betrayals, but it does not frighten us: it all simply does not matter. Everything is nothing. Christ alone is everything: and his Mother Mary bears him, with the hands of a sister and the caresses of a Virgin Mother.

3 May – As a Christian I seem to have failed. But may the Lord give me the strength to cope with my failure in a Christian way. What vanity is mine! I want to have outward satisfactions and not suffer inwardly. Reality is the Cross.

Silence. Suffering. And may they pass over me as over a mule-track in the country, without consideration.

You always rebel against suffering, forgetting that your pain distils joy for the Mystical Body, that your destruction serves for the construction of the Church.

1 October – Why does Mary play such an important part amongst us? Because amongst us those who truly follow the Gospel feel and behave as children, to whom their mother is everything and serves every purpose: she is sought after because she introduces them to God. They take her by the hand, hang on to her clothes, in order that she may lead them to the Father. There is no more reassuring, no more loving or beautiful way of presenting oneself to him. And then, in the company of one's Mother, one's whole life is more beautiful: nature laughs and men themselves do not seem savage any longer.

11 November – Our life is drawn behind the changeable drive of the will, which, as though testing its balance, overturns now on the right, now on the left. How happy it is if it discovers that its natural position is in adapting itself to the Will of God: in willing what God wills. Then the spirit is at peace.

Even the weight of sin serves, in restrospect, a useful purpose, for it acts as a ballast to the balloon of the vanity which forces us to rise.

14 November – There are two angles from which to contemplate the human tragedy without despairing and rejecting life in society, without growing morose, but rather deriving joy and peace from it: charity and death. Seen from the standpoint of charity the tragedy is eased, seen from the standpoint of death it disappears. Science, politics, art, social relations, lose some of their savagery and their power to intimidate if they are seen in relation to death or if the men who practise them are considered with the warmth of love. Love and death, the men of old used to say, coupling them as the two ultimate realities.

15 November – The edifices of certain charitable institutions, with their high walls and protruding bossed stones, intersected by barred windows and their sumptuous entrances, closed at meal times and bolted and barred at night, give the impression of a charity that has become petrified, walled up, something dead. Those defences do not keep out only thieves, they keep the poor out too. Inside, people's hearts also are barricaded behind shutters, locking themselves up apprehensively at meal times and during the hours of sleep, when the poor ask for a crust of bread and the homeless would be glad of a passage in which the wind did not whistle and the snow did nor whirl. However, do not you, who take scandal thus, bolt and bar your house in the same way, whereas it too ought to be a temple? And do you not lock your heart up, whereas it too ought to be wide open? When love is lacking, life freezes, it calcifies: it becomes death.

6 December – What a lesson this ministerial crisis is, these conferences of the Three, of the Five, and this feverish activity on the part of professors, journalists, politicians and economists. Mere busy-bodies . . . the reality which is discovered beneath the hysterics and all the talk is that truth which our mystics used to assert: everything is nothing. God alone.

All is nought. God alone.

26 December – The Church does not die because its soul is charity; and charity is God in her.

Either one depends on God or on men. God then is our freedom in regard to men and to depend on God is to cling to the sources of life and joy.

1946

20 January – The mere fact that as soon as one disaster is remedied two more, ten more arrive, demonstrates the precarious and provisional nature of our sojourn on the planet. The fact that no agreement can be reached on the elementary reasons for men's living in fellowship means that we are made for living in fellowship with God. God makes the precariousness of life on earth and social life amongst men tolerable. The proof of it is purgatory.

Charity prevents truth from becoming proud and making itself an instrument and pretext for absolutism and intransigence. Truth, with charity. This is the blood which gives the brain purity and youth.

13 March – History is a novel with a key which opens eternity and the reality of this earth: because if God is taken away nothing at all remains: because God is all.

5 April – Can a politician be a saint? Can a saint be a politician? Test the answer to the question on yourself now that you are becoming a politician.

13 April – It could be said that the important thing is not the conquest of holiness but the effort to attain it. But it is all the same: to be holy means to endeavour to be holy. And therefore falls do not dishearten you: the important thing is to get up again and make a fresh start. The definitive conquest takes place in the Church Triumphant.

20 April – I am not afraid of you because I love you! This is what one must be able to say to one's brothers in the guise of adversaries. Overcome fear: the inferiority complex is the stature of Satan; and rise to love, which makes us ready to serve and is the human level: the level of man redeemed by God, son of his Creator.

2 August – Spreading sanctity by a poor sheet of newspaper, spreading sanctity from a lobby of forlorn hopes; . . . who will perform this miracle?

9 December – The human illusion plays between two mirages: one set in the plans of the past, the other situated in the gardens of the future. With the first, we imagine nostalgically a time in which life was better (in peace, freedom, comfort); with the second, a better regime is anticipated, to be realised in accordance with our ideals. Between the two dreams we, for our part, carry the Cross and our life is spent as an ascent to Calvary. Blessed the man who accepts it in the spirit of expiation! Blessed the man who sets his heart on the fulfilments of the next world: where there will be peace and love and justice without end! In the meantime, we must work to repel evil as far as we can and to help our brothers.

20 December – The important thing is to sanctify everything that has to do with us: thought and clothes, love and sex, work and money, democracy and liberty: all of them good things if holy, all of them condemned to be perverted if deprived of the Holy Spirit.

26 December – Take care that your life is not a unique opportunity lost: the opportunity offered you to sanctify yourself. At least use these few days, or few hours, that are left.

1947

22 April – I must raise all my affections on high, to a level of light: put them on the Lady Altar, like a display of flowers, to honour her and sanctify me.

29 April – This suffering and this humiliation serve to demolish the superstructure of vanity within which the true person is hidden and to put us back, naked souls, facing you. But, Lord, strike me and save my children.

4 May – If everyone abandons us it is in order that we may remain alone, you and I. You, the All, I the nought. But how good it is to entrust my nothingness to your totality! Then I feel that I am being deified.

And if I am brought down to the depths of abasement, in humiliation, it is in order that I may see you in all your infinite greatness. But how good it is to rise, for love of you, from the depths of humiliation up to your height! Then I feel that I am being admitted to Paradise.

All this that to the eyes of the world is misfortune becomes thus a destruction of tinsel and of compromises: half-achievements and half-measures: a return to the simple and the definitive.

13 May – The play of love and the yoke of humility: the dialectic of the spiritual life. By the former we bear God within us, by the latter we raise ourselves towards God.

But do not refuse humiliations: do not rebel against them. Thank the Lord who allows them to come: they are a sign that he remembers you, that he makes you like himself – who was spat upon and given gall to drink and numbered amongst evil-doers.

25 June – I lack patience, which is the rock base on which the different forms of adversity are blunted.

I lack love, which is the intelligence of the heart, and for which intrigues, ambitions, hypocrisy and cunning are straw.

I lack faith, in virtue of which even if everyone were to fail in loyalty to religion and morality I should calmly go ahead.

All this lack comes from the fact that the clatter of money and ambitions, with the shadows that are cast by them, drowns the voice of God and dims the vision of spiritual things for me. Surrounded by that actuality the soul wastes away through exhaustion.

Here indeed there is need of revolution.

Every time that bitterness takes possession of me over my failures in politics, literature or social life, I fall. I fall beneath the level of the most elementary requirements of Christian ascesis. In envy I die, in vanity I agonize.

3 July – You are experiencing what you already knew, and that is that if you lower life beneath the level of religion it falls into a region of cold and darkness, it enters into death, where it decomposes in dejection and fury, to the extent of breeding worms: a life that becomes wholly vermiculation: a factory of death. Restore it to the region of faith, to the warmth of charity, and it is re-invigorated, regains light and again produces joy.

11 September – For the rest, I consider that what matters is to become a saint. To be an apostle of the diffusion of Christ in the world around one. The opportunity to become holy is offered by the trials that God sends. He sends them for this purpose, but they are wasted. I waste them, by rebelling, considering them almost as a wrong, as if God owed us sweetmeats in exchange for a few feeble prayers. We look upon these trials then as betrayals, and indeed they are, but they are our betrayals of God.

Incomprehension, slander, contempt and scorn: that is the raw material out of which we build sanctity, if we fuse them in the fire of charity, with the wisdom of humility.

The very moment that you make contact with God, peace and joy stream into your soul, and in its happiness it sighs with St. Paul: I desire to be dissolved and to be with Christ.

14 October – The thought of death chills the man who does not think about it. But in fact, if we look it in the face, we see that it enlightens and brings peace. Placed at the boundary of the Eternal and the contingent, it casts on the next life a reflection of light which brings serenity, a breath of air which purifies. Here below, existence is cluttered up with all the parasitic vegetation of illusions, ambitions, traps, annoying and poisonous swarms of insects. Then wealth and honours appear in their poverty of dry bones and flesh that has rotted away. And the full value of love is seen. One sees that to live is to love: and that to hate is to die. Freed from those wrappings, existence becomes easy once again. That means that the thought of death gives life its meaning.

10 November – Lord, draw me up to you: right up to the level of your Cross: so that, with you, I may from that height look at the earth in a spirit of sacrifice, give myself to my brothers and offer myself to the Father: and thus associate myself with your offering, and in it, through you, divine Victim, earn the forgiveness of the Judge.

21 December – By the fact of having been born I belong to God. In virtue of having been created I participate in the nature of the Creator: I am of his lineage and I bear the image and likeness of him. And in virtue of the fact that I bear in me the impress of the Creator, the man who sees me sees him imaged. Thus, while it is impossible for man to grasp the entire essence of the divinity, he can grasp some likeness of it with the naked eye and at every step, by recalling this truth. In such a way, every rational creature is God imaged: each creature is the authorised representation of the King of the world, in a foreign land, a land of pilgrimages. And not a purely external representation but one of intrinsic value, connected, by bonds of sonship and the relationship arising from creation, with the Father and Creator, who is also Judge and Master: so that, in social relationships, with God entering in as initial and final term, the good done to one's brother goes to stay in God, who rewards it as done to himself, and the evil done to one's brother makes its impact on his person and is punished by him, as done to him. Dealing then with my brother I am dealing with God, through the intermediary of a third person.

By baptism I am incorporated into the Body of Christ; I become a member of Christ, living substance of him: I am Christ, in part, mystically.

The sacraments and the graces accompany the Spirit of God in me, so that my body comes to me from him, my spirit is redeemed by Christ, is infused with the Holy Spirit. That is the way in which through the Incarnation, as St. Augustine puts it, God became man in order that man might become God.

The Eucharist, in particular, infuses into my arteries the very Blood of Christ, so as to make me his blood relation.

My task as a Christian is to build up Christ in me. To the extent that he grows in me, my ego diminishes. I must diminish in order that he may grow, as the Baptist said. And as he grows, love grows: as I diminish, selfishness diminishes.

This way my personality is not annulled. Rather, it is Christified. It grows until it is deified, identifying itself with him. And the identification is complete when I can say: It is not I who live but Christ who lives in me.

I offer the container, the temple, but he who lives in it is Christ, as on the altar. I offer my will, but I make of my personality the raw material for building up Christ within me. When he has been built up I can say henceforward: I am another Christ (*alter Christus*). It is tremendous, incomprehensible: I am Christ. Perhaps, a poor Christ, but such that through me, through my actions and words, almost as if the Word had become incarnate again in me, Christ expresses himself to the world.

Thus the Incarnation is continued.

Such a divine result cannot be a cause of pride for man, because it is not owing to him, it is owing to Christ: rather the worth of a man is in proportion to the extent that he is not himself but allows Christ to be in him.

Such a result on the other hand, confers on the poor human creature a divine dignity and at the same time an evangelical responsibility – that of evangelising, so as to make the Gospel understood and welcomed in the measure that others see it incarnate in him.

And thus my vocation is accomplished; and the rule of conduct is found: there is no problem as to my place in the world. I am Christ, in image. *Alter Christus,* another Christ. Life, public and private, becomes a con-formation to the Gospel: a conformation to Christ. That is my royal priesthood: my union with God.

This clothes me in humility, in the gratitude of the nought that is made infinite, and it lavishes upon me serenity and strength and rectitude: but at the same time, it imposes on me a superhuman duty and if I were to fail in that duty I would be, like Judas, a trader in the Redemption.

Lord, take me to yourself and give me yourself: let it not be I who live but you who live in me.

30 December – But if it is so, if I am *alter Christus,* another Christ, if Christ lives in me, if the Trinity dwells in me, how could I any longer experience fear in a terrifying world or feel saddened in a system built out of hatred or be troubled at the mediocrity that prevails all round me or concern myself with a future which selfishness and malice are clogging up with horrors?

If I am a temple occupied by the Holy Spirit, how can I be subject to the spirit of the world, which occupies brains and intestines for purely sensorial functions?

I have joy and I give joy. I have the Faith and I spread faith. I have peace and I fight for peace. I have God and I can do all in his omnipotence.

1948

1 January – Outside love stretches the ocean of stupidity.

23 January – Go out of love and you enter into criminality. You enter into disorder and hell begins. For love is the atmosphere of Paradise where the Godhead is the air you breathe. If you put man between Christ and yourself, Christ appears to you in darkness, deformed; if you put Christ between man and yourself, man appears divinised.

On the other side of a veil of the spirit is God. It is enough to recollect oneself for a moment to feel the breath of God.

On the other side of a veil, the veil of the flesh, is Satan: it is enough to be distracted for a moment to feel his flame.

You believe that you have interposed a manifold wall of meditations, prayers, resolutions, and all at once you discover that the Enemy is on the watch, like a dog, and the moment you turn your head, he jumps at your back and sinks his fangs into you, taking you by surprise. You believe that he is far away and he is present. You believe that you are fortified and you are ever weak, because you are ever in the flesh; which perspires through a thousand pores and is highly vulnerable; so that to the last moment you can never dispense yourself from being on your guard.

Between you and sin there is a thin diaphragm. Between life and hell, which is death, there is stretched only a curtain, which a breath of air moves. It is well for you if God's grace, breathing, holds you in again.

The solitude that is fearsome is not that of the hermits: but that of public squares, of social gatherings and at times that of one's own associates when one is involved with them only to be ignored and misunderstood, rejected and thrown out, as an encumbrance, because of the space which one occupies, the air that one breathes, the life that one is leading.

The catacombs are not our lot: but it may fall to each one of us to live beneath a mound of contempt and incomprehension, and to be worn down by persecution.

10 February – How pleasant suffering becomes when the thought of Jesus enters into it. Then one feels that one is included in that process of production of merits, beneath the press of suffering, thanks to which the Church is built up. And so to rebel against pain is to shirk the task of building up the Mystical Christ. For sufferings are the birthpangs of the Mystical Christ in the world.

Because you go to Mass you believe yourself dispensed from the efforts of the trial in which God purifies you.

Because they slandered you and offended you in your very practice of religion and morality, you considered yourself as it were injured by God's justice, as if your due was only praise and recognition; you forget that Christ was slandered and struck with a reed.

And so, rebelling angrily, you have fallen like the man who is furthest away from the things of God; and you have thought of running away to escape the trial, as if you were owed some special treatment in the divine economy with regard to mankind. But the charge is: to suffer, not to flee. And to suffer without losing peace, defending your peace within a shelter, built with your love and your work: a shelter which will remain standing even if your house collapses.

29 June – The fate of the fruit tree bears some resemblance to man's lot, bearing fruit in due season. While it flowers there is birdsong and chirruping around the tree, warm winds and sunshine; and while it brings its apples to ripeness the whole of nature in a veritable orgy wraps it in warmth. Then its cultivators retire into their farmhouses and kitchens and after some brief show of life and colour in the autumn cold silence takes over, under a leaden sky, bringing the leaves, like last tears, down on to the dry ground. And so it happens to man, when he has passed the age of maximum yield. Delusions and friendships fall like leaves, an enveloping silence reigns and the countryside becomes mournful: he is left gradually all alone to contemplate, as a mute spectator, the progress of his own dissolution.

None-the-less, just as in that cold and in that solitude, the tree is preparing for the new spring, gathering warmth and sap, so can man make of that winter ebb of friends and strength the gathering of a vigour fraught with a new existence: he can use that desertion by men to cling to God, to fill up that decline of the human element with divine grace: and then, within the silence that has been intensified to gigantic proportions by ingratitude and avarice, over his wasted and cold old age, he can fill himself with the warmth of God, mount inwardly to the extent that he sinks outwardly, and yield men a harvest which is not reckoned by economics but is calculated by theology. In Man's winter God's spring begins.

14 July – And what else does 'making a mistake' mean in human relationships but failing in love? Augustine had penetrated to the kernel of Christianity when he saw that the man who loves does not err. The man who errs is the man who does not love. In a word, the matter always comes back to this: love is the form that truth assumes in the feelings: and truth is the form which love takes in the intellect; and truth–love is the same as life, since it is the Spirit of God, which is life. We wish to conduct our politics without regard to this reality, and what happens is that they continually come to grief, just as health, when the body is fed with ersatz foods, deteriorates in every respect. And to the extent that a man separates himself from love, he approaches death, by the road of hatred, violence, falsehood: all these violations of truth–love.

How human man is when he is asleep! He takes on then so often, an aspect of suffering, as it were a prelude to death. Then the mask is dropped and man is left naked: a small being thrown into a muddle that is too much for him. In that distress, when every covering has fallen off, man recovers his humanity, that which is his reality, his truth, often buried under layers of falsehood, which is Satan's make-up. When on a sultry afternoon, you find those combative men, divided by passions and hypocrisies, sunk in sleep on the sofas of Monte Citorio*, you see them all disposed in attitudes of stress, made equal by the same suffering of the human condition. Oppositions and differences have flowed into a Lethe of pain which is the liquid of peace produced for others by those very men.

When things are looked at from the high vantage point of death, an immaculate summit which dominates them all, they resume their several places in due order: some which appeared to be distant become close again; others which appeared to be near, retire to a distance: large things are deflated; tiny things grow to gigantic proportions. Like actors dressed up to play a part (Chrystosom's idea!) human beings take off their costumes and greasepaint and return to their everyday reality. This return to proper proportions and situations could chill the heart, as the back-stage of a theatre does where the actors are washing off their greasepaint, the sham mountains are piled up in a corner and jewels and lights are laid aside amidst broken glass: life then could seem like a polar landscape, a funeral parlour, such as would warrant the disgust of certain existentialists; then upon that bare and mournful landscape there must be brought the virginal smile of Mary, and at once it is lighted up and given fresh warmth, it clothes itself in beauty and joy in which life flowers like a perennial spring, which is Christ in the midst of us.

---

* The Italian House of Commons.

1 August – The ultimate reason why you go wrong is that while you impose a Christian rule on your life, you then wish to follow methods other than those of holiness; thus you create a discord from which disappointment and failure come to you. Either seek the happiness of the spirit or seek outward power. The two things cannot be reconciled. Happiness is the product of interior freedom: it is *spernere se, sperni**: that is freedom.

A religion that becomes political. A religion that becomes metallic. A religion that becomes erotic. There you have the contradiction which Satan brings into play, making a Pharisee of the Christian.

Praised be the Lord. Praised be the Blessed Virgin.

Praised be St. Gemma (Galgani); my brother, my Mother, my sister, who live with me in this study. They have never betrayed me: never disappointed me. The more I have been alone the more they have kept my company; and with their sober graciousness they have always inspired me with great joy. Without them even in the midst of relations and friends, how would I not be left alone – alone like a traveller in the desert which has no end.

5 August – All these clamours, from political meetings and assemblies, all this frenzy of ambitions and intrigues, all these anxieties over disasters and over trifles, will sink into silence, wrapped in darkness, as soon as death comes; and a like obscurity will reduce to equality great men and small, enemies and friends, nature and memory. The antipathies by which we are torn, the ideologies for which we disquiet ourselves, the impostures and the conventions, the rhetoric and the treachery, all will collapse into nothing, dissolving, in an instant into nought; hell will be the great rubbish dump where all those forms of

---

* Imitation of Christ (II. 12, 9) – "To despise oneself and to be despised".

evildoing will be heaped up: and where they will ferment into gases poisonous to the soul which, at least in death, has not freed itself in God.

And vice-versa, the sufferings, the humble sighs, the desires to do good, the loaves given with a smile to the poor, all the good deeds and reflexions carried out amidst the press of hatreds and hypocrisies, all this humble production of good, through the miracle of death, will grow into eternal life, will mount into the light, will take on the breadth of the rainbow, drawing furrows of light across the immense purity of the heavens.

Thus death is the crisis which settles all: the violent shift of scene: a changing of the guard which reverses positions, since it brings into the kingdom of the anonymous crowds, feeble creatures, the unknown servants of the human family, the victims of sacrifice, people tried by suffering and love. It is the great act of justice, in which the screens and the curtains of wealth and imposture will be swept away by a burst of flame, laying bare the ugliness that has not been seen and at the same time the beauty that has gone unnoticed.

Love, like fire, tends to mount on high, eager to return to God, from whom it comes forth. Flaming only towards the heights, to embrace all creatures, it must begin from the bottom: begin from ground level in order to soar towards the blue of the heavens. The more it begins from the bottom and the more souls it embraces, the more of the world it possesses. And since it is made concrete in service, in order to serve, it puts itself beneath the most abject human being, so that not even he may withdraw himself from the warmth of love.

For this reason humility is needed, which is putting oneself on the *humus*, on the ground, upsetting all stools and footrests, and all the multifarious objects which enable one to get on top. The man who gets on top rejects someone or something: in that 'some person' there is a representation of God, something divine: so that the prouder a man becomes, that is, gets on top, the more he impoverishes himself. The saint's ambition does not reject anything: it tends to envelop in its love all creatures, like St. Francis, imitator of Christ, and therefore, it dilates the soul and conquers heaven to the extent that it humbles itself. In a word, humility is a position of conquest, it belongs to the heroes of charity.

To put oneself beneath all: a condition for loving – serving – all.

A simplifying position, in which intrigues, pressures and quarrels have no play: the man who puts himself down there is left in peace, in the transparent atmosphere which precedes sin; the sin of worldly ambitions and of money, power and lust. Wickedness is mediocre: and it stays in mid-air: it does not reach heaven any more than it touches the earth: it has no height because it lacks a base. It is cessation from good.

For every beautiful woman that you meet, recite a Hail Mary; so you thank God for her beauty; you contemplate femininity in the light of the Blessed Virgin; and you purify your senses from every vain image.

Spernere se, sperni (to despise oneself, to be despised). That is freedom. That is happiness. You on the other hand seek your reward here below: you do good in order to have the esteem of men; you cultivate virtue in order to be paid for it. You are worse than the pagans: you are the most wretched of traders.

The Christian is *alter Christus* (another Christ): and therefore you must expect spittle and derision and the judgment which puts you beneath the feet of a robber, which kills you amidst cries of "Long Live Barabbas!"

You are always looking for praise from outside: you live for it. It drains you, and it distracts you from your interior life, and keeps you absorbed in an anxious scheming to win applause and petty rewards, in the fine dust of gossip; in the bustle of lobbies and chambers, in conferences and hotels. And so you lose yourself and you lose others. You are pulled apart by the wind that descends from the roofs, by the dust that swirls through the streets, by the death of which vain things are unceasingly dying.

16 August – You cling to life as fiercely as if you were trying to have a quarter of it to live over again even after your death, by binding youself to memories, fame and gratitude. And you find that your time is overcast with clouds of fear: fears that new invasions may submerge, along with Europe, your own titles to remembrance and gratitude, the things that are dear to you and the persons connected with you. And this thought, which is a possibility, brings home to you the precariousness of all: it is a lecture on the Imitation of Christ given from a chair of pestilence and explosives.

17 September – This morning, at Montecitorio, I was called upon by angels: a Capuchin, a Friar Minor, a Conventual Franciscan, a man and woman belonging to the Third Order: the woman was Silvia Lubig★ *(sic!)* who is launching a community at Trent.

24 September – There is no need, Lord, for me to tell over again the catalogue of my needs, endless as it is.
It is enough that I need you.

24 October – If the spectacle of human meanness disquiets you, contemplate the majesty of God.
And if humanity appears ugly, restore your eyes by contemplating God.

11 November – Does faith falter? Then open the valve of love and that will refresh it with oxygen. Does love languish? Then gather the remains into the mould of faith

---

★ The meeting was with Chiara Lubich, foundress of the Focolare Movement. Silvia is her baptismal name.

and that will rejuvenate it. Are you weary of life? Then think of death. And if the company of men exhaust you, insert yourself into the communion of saints and this tangle of ambitions and careers, treachery and agitation, will appear to you as a trap laid for your happiness and you will have nothing to do with it.

20 November – This fit of anger which has exploded resembles the explosion of a little compressed gas in a container: it is the rupture of a little brain filled with burning fumes. This always happens because things and persons are not put in their proper station, which is a modest station of change and of becoming nothing: a display of shadows which the approaching evening engulfs. Always because one does not remember that there is nothing serious but God and salvation in him: and all the rest is nothing and warrants only a smile tinged with pity; humanity's hubbubs, shadowy representations on the screen, a destruction of atoms which think themselves important. This is what life is: a brief comedy which clutters up the space in which one's conversation with God must be conducted. To attend to men, to their humours, angers, threats, betrayals, to be surprised that when you do good to them they despise you, that when fed they requite you with spittle, is like dropping the ladder which mounts to paradise on shifting mud, or on a surface of withered leaves covering a lake's heavy waters. What is man's task? The whole world is in the power of the Evil One. And this realistic pessimism supports hope, gives the measure of the immeasurable; while the treachery of human beings arouses love for God and loyalty to him. What are you surprised at? Man produces more evil than good; and often even the good is vitiated by a wrong intention; out of love he makes people suffer; and he unleashes wars, famines and massacres for an Ideal or with the intention of doing good. Master this senselessness and weakness, by laughing wisely over it. To grow angry is to fall beneath that weakness, to enslave oneself to that misery, to plunge into senselessness.

22 November – Anyone who humiliates you is your friend. The secret of the economy of morality is to endure incomprehension, fits of anger and insults gladly, first from persons close at hand, then from those at a distance.

28 November – Man is an instrument for suffering. And for making others suffer.

I wish to offer my sufferings to Christ, enclosing them in the silence with which I wish to counter cruel words. I wish to give love for hatred, forgiveness for revenge, intelligence for instinct: I will not let myself be overcome by the weakness of the violent.

Jesus said to Blessed Angela of Foligno: "You will know that I am in you when, if someone outrages and hurts you, you not only endure it with patience but also feel a lively desire for outrages and sufferings and consider them when they come, as a grace. This is the most certain sign of God." (The Wonderful Visions).*

N B.

True – and this is where *I* fall most easily and betray grace.

Pride is an outward expansion to compensate for an inward contraction.

18 December – At 2.30 this morning I took an aeroplane of the Brazilian Pan Air Line at Ciampino and after a flight of five hours I reached Lisbon, to which I had been invited by the newspaper *Novidades*. At Lisbon I spoke in the hall of the Geographical Society to an assembly of three thousand persons, including the Cardinal Patriarch and eighteen bishops. I spoke about Catholic journalism, in Portuguese. The following morning I was at Fatima.

---

* L'esperienza di Dio Amore by Angela da Foligno, Città Nuova, Roma, 1973.

Yesterday evening I had half an hour's conversation with Salazar, the Head of the Government. Speaking of the governments of various European countries, he sagely concluded: "Until the people grow tired of us".

1949

4 January – Lord, I ask you for health, intelligence, strength, wealth, love, satisfactions, a healthy family, happiness on earth and paradise in heaven: and in return I give you distractions, coldness, doubts, lies, compromises with lust and luxury, base passions, wretchedness and treachery.

And there are millions of people who do the same as I. So that our barter is this: we bring polluted waste and you give purity: we contribute the rubbish of death, you offer gifts of life; we sell what is ugly and you bestow what is beautiful. And thus unceasingly you purify and smile: you are the love which revives, like an eternal oxygen, the anaemic globules of our social organism.

Protect mind and heart; within a strong-box or a diving suit: in order that fear may not get at them and envy may not slip in; that the deadly mould of rancour may not be deposited there; that pessimism may not make them rusty. Grant that avarice may not take root there; but above all that hatred may not spring up there. The intellect needs a clear atmosphere: light and space. The heart needs warmth: love and happiness. And love makes happiness. Give me the art of loving: and of loving when I am beginning to hate.

The thought comes to me that that bitter chalice from which Christ's humanity recoiled, was full of all the sufferings with which the whole of society before and after the Redemption ought to have expiated its sins. The expiation taken on by him for all had to be the sum of the expiation owed by each one. A suffering without

41

end: all the suffering of humanity concentrated in one cup: a cup of gall, therefore, bitter beyond anything man could imagine.

30 January – What importance is accorded to this adventure, tragic buffoonery as it is! Books complicate it, interests mask it, gunfire cuts it short. . . . It is worth the trouble of being lived if one succeeds in transforming it into a loving adventure. An adventure of love, in which God is present.

To die to the world, to die to oneself. The effect resembles physical death. Like it, it leads to a liberation from the daily assault of evil, it puts us beyond its grasp; it liberates us. But not for a cessation of life, much rather for a completion of it: for God puts himself in the place of the ego and then life assumes giant proportions. Once God is in us, who is against us?

It is always a question of liberation; of redemption, and thereby, freeing ourselves from the Evil One, we leave him with a shadow in his hands.

10 February – Yesterday in the Chamber of Deputies, I spoke on the occasion of the centenary of the Roman Republic and sketched a profile of Mazzini from the Catholic point of view. The subject was rather a difficult one for a Catholic but I received congratulations for my speech from Catholics, Republicans, Socialists and Monarchists.

27 February – Tonadico – I have been given this Word of Life: "Jesus I wish to be yours: yours as you think best: do with me all that you wish."

1951

9 July – Ama nesciri et pro nihilo reputari.★
Be the buried seed: hidden and put in its place: thus you
will bear fruit.
Kill your own will.
Do not seek consolations.
Do not lament.
Thus you win God: your freedom. There is only the
wisdom of the Cross;
I have resolved to die
And what happens does not matter any longer to me;
Now I wish to disappear.

In the abandoned heart of Jesus
All this toiling
With avarice and for vanity
Disappears in love:
I have recovered my freedom.

I have resolved to die
By this death which does not die any more;
Now I wish to enjoy
With God his eternal youth.

1954

17 July – People who drift through life . . . People who
kill time . . . And instead time is the precious endow-
ment which is meant for consuming our life: consuming
it like a taper before an ikon. Living is being consumed
as a holocaust to God, being destroyed, bit by bit, like
the victims of the Old Law: consummating the Passion
and Death in a longer or shorter space of time. Life
becomes this sacrifice, this slow combustion on the altar

★ Love to be unknown and reckoned as nought – Imitation of
Christ. I, 2 and 3.

of holocausts, naturally, if it is accompanied by prayer: if it is wholly interwoven with prayer. A sacrifice without prayer is a gesture without any soul: it is useless. Without prayer – an assiduous sighing to him, thinking of him, becoming him – life is not lived: it is dead. It is drifting through life . . . a killing of time instead of putting the old man to death.

Putting oneself, the old man, to death, the consuming of self like fuel that gradually burns away, is a liberation of a new life, a rebirth, a true birth to true Life, to God.

21 August – At times, even the apostle, after having served his brothers for years suffers crises of distrust and no longer believes in men. Perhaps it is only a lesson from God teaching him that God alone is trustworthy. From the hosannas to the "Crucify him"! the road is short. Amidst the breakdown of things and consciences, he alone remains: Christ Crucified.

Live in a mad world like a contemplative. As if in an enclosure. Not enclosed between four walls, but enclosed in the heart of Jesus. Be consecrated: not belonging any longer to yourself, but to God. To God alone. And do everything in him, with him, so that all you do is a divine operation or divinised, even everything that God allows, even the sufferings, which are all accepted as the will of God.

Be immolated: enclosed; dead to the world. Although a layman, be a religious in your soul; consecrated, offered to the Lord, like an anvil, practising the evangelical counsels as far as is possible – poverty, obedience, chastity – will provoke the anger of Satan and of men; amidst the humiliation of misunderstandings, say, gladly, crucified on the Cross with Christ Crucified: *Bonum mihi est quia humiliasti me* (It is good for me that you have humiliated me), as the Psalmist puts it.

Do not spend this one life you have in gathering pennies or power or some other vanity: spend it as a light that burns on Christ's altar.

Let every deed and every word be love; including breathing, including work, together with each human relationship, let it be love, even if with him, crucified Love, you have to cry out: "My God, My God, why have you forsaken me?"

26 September – This cult of the ego which installs itself in the place of God, is carried to the point of decadence. Even amidst the turmoil of dramatic events, you will find that, above the tears and the cries and the general anguish there stands out, like wreckage in a storm, this fixation of the ego, this maniac idolatry of one's own being, of one's own interests, this foolish colossus, filled up with air of one's own self; and the universal is lost, love is lost, for terror and the fear of a miserly, mean and stifled cult of one's own non-being.

May God pluck me away from the old man in me, this wreckage from a deluge of sin: may he give me hatred for it and enable me to forget it so that I may no longer see anything but him both in himself and in my brothers, his image, and in nature, the projection of him.

14 October – Ultimately it is a question of this: of not refusing the gifts of the Father. This sums up everything. The simplicity of God.

14 November – You keep God in your head always, as far as words are concerned. But deeds? In fact, you are always talking with your own god, with your fantasies, with creatures. If you accomplish the revolution of making yourself talk, in love, and obedience, with God, you along with him alone, then you have attained the unitive way, in which you advance in a Calvary which is a Paradise.

27 December – I am in the present with my heart in the future. I live stretched out towards that nought in which

I long for liberation from the stresses of the present moment, in order to find the conditions in which to begin the climb to God.

Deceived! Unseeing! The conditions for climbing to the Eternal belong precisely to the present moment, just as this unfolds itself from instant to instant; they consist in straits and trials and torments, in the air pockets and the deep abysses in which I find myself from moment to moment. This cross is the condition for being with Christ; for uniting myself to him there, nailed, myself, here: both of us a holocaust on one and the same Cross, for the one Redemption, I, even I, associated by his love, with his Passion. In this absence of peace and failure to find love, in this madness brought on by the cares of every pause, I am anguished, troubled, breath-less, having to live as if dying, always in a way that is distasteful to me – here is my Cross, the ladder to the Resurrection, Jesus abandoned on the Cross! Instability is my stability, uncertainty is my foundation, death here is my life there.

16 February – To sanctify oneself not for oneself, nor for others, but for God: for to sanctify oneself means to become a saint, to become the Holy One, who is God, by means of transformation into him, a transformation which, under the working of grace, is achieved by tearing oneself from oneself, driving out one's ego and filling oneself up with God. In this process it is necessary to shun even the created beings who are dearest and purest and holiest in order to look only at him, then, in him they will be found again, nearer and dearer.

The way is interrupted and, at times, delayed by falls: by falling from God to the ego: by the resurgence of the old man, who blocks the view. And then nothing is seen any longer and one wavers towards the idolatry of one's own self, and one begins to complain, exhibiting oneself to the heavens as a victim. However if it is no longer I who live but Christ who lives in me, there is no longer any room for falls and laments: for Christ is always the same: and if, on the Cross, for a moment he believed himelf abandoned *immediately* he turned to the Father in trust: *In manus tuas* . . . (Into your hands . . .).

But in order that Christ may live in me, it is necessary that my thinking should be his thinking, my feeling and my willing his feeling and his willing: and he expresses will and thought and feeling for me through the gospels, and through the Saints, through my Superiors and through his inspirations. I renounce myself and I recover you, God: you take me, and I will take you: and the exchange is immense.

3 September – If universal history is a fifth Gospel for humanity, the course of each individual's life is the same thing for him. Seen from God's point of view it appears as a plan for bringing us back from dispersion to unity with him. One sees then how detachment from the persons dear to one and the loss of honours and position are a clearance of human elements in order to launch you, alone with God alone. And then every day takes on the value of a divine adventure if it is used to make you mount along the sun's ray – your ray, the one which connects with the Sun that is God. It is spoken of as a journey towards death; and it is progress towards freedom on the summit of which the Father awaits you: therefore a journey towards life, a life which never has any end.

19 September – These homeward steps, tired, beneath the sun and the rain, are the return journey to your house, O Father, in the same way that these toils, cares, debts and irritations of every kind and degree, all the day long and the sicknesses and physical exhaustion by which the body is being broken down are the dissolution of matter in order to arrive at your Kingdom, O Son; and all these pains are my collaboration in the sacrifice of the cross and become drops of blood, of your blood, since you give them value and assimilate them to the outcome of your holocaust; and this yearning for return, this hunger for the divine, this need for sanctification, is a participation in your gifts, O Holy Spirit. And thus, I am in a tram or in my office or on the road and I am in the cycle of your life, O Most Holy Trinity: you bear me in you, I bear you in me; and, as I draw closer to physical death, I grow in you, mounting through the passes of the mystical ascent. Thus this wearisome, monotonous and dreary thing which is life in old age becomes a youthful liberation, a winged leap into the Eternal, into the midst of your Sun, O uncreated Trinity, to the side of Mary and the Saints, of Paul and Augustine, and Francis and Clare and Catherine and Teresa . . . to this jubilation of souls, who do not die.

1956

12 January – You can stay on your feet, even if everyone abandons you: it is enough to lean on the Cross.

The Cross keeps you on your feet; and leaning against it you find yourself suddenly side by side with so many others, whom the Cross supports: unfortunate creatures and Saints, rich and poor, young and old, the living and the dead. You find yourself, around Christ, incorporated in the universal Church, taken up into solidarity with the angels and the saints: welcomed into the arms of God.

This is not an ascent of the years: it is an ascent towards God. To grow old is to come closer to him: a growth towards his eternity; a liberation of self for his youth.

In this ascent conversation becomes dialogue; talking with men blossoms into talk with God. For he alone remains; and face to face with him, the soul: *solus cum sola*. Illnesses create silence all around one; the years thin one's friends: the world falls away like a withered fruit. The very souls who loved us in God plan to meet us again outside this world in him; Existence unfolds like a clearance operation of all that is human, in order to prepare us, as clean stones, to build up Christ. The soul itself, while it loses everything, yearns to lose even itself, in order that it may give room to him.

In this development the significance of history is grasped: a process of liberation from the fleeting, for love of the Eternal: a collaboration of nature and of men with the Redemption. Mortification, disappointments, betrayals, illness, desertion . . . are the pruning of the tree for the new Spring, which will produce flowers in heaven. Thus history is a sacred history: the return journey of individuals and of society from exile to the Fatherland. Thus life is like a corridor which gradually becomes dark and silent, and at the end of it he who waits: Love which would have the soul, the Bride, for Itself.

There is no need to seek out solitude: it is enough to accept the solitude that society creates around us, abandoning ourselves on the threshold of the temple, in which God is waiting. Alone with God: there we are with life.

13 March – Why faith? A covering of thick darkness and gleaming lights, behind which God hides himself. We see him solely *in aenigmate* (in a riddle): we see him through faith. The logic of this darkening is understandable, it is a defence, since we cannot see, with our eyes, even the midday sun: and God is a sun without any limitation. But the darkening causes suffering, bristling with doubts as it is.

When we come to think of it, faith appears as the correlative of freedom. He has given us this divine greatness: he desires in return this human humility. Looked at in this way, believing is seen to be a re-ascent to meet him, to reach the face to face vision of him: a preparation, a training and as it were a process of equalising which moves from below towards him who descends from the peaks of light.

12 October – The divine adventure of being in the world yet deserting it in the spirit. *Kalos ho kindunos, tou automolein pros theon:* it is a fine risk to desert to God. To tear oneself from the pomps of vanity: to become a servant, disappear into the dark: to be reckoned a nought: to become a docile instrument of divine action amongst one's brothers. To renounce one's own will and become, through obedience, God's will. To renounce money and wealth and through poverty to become free.

19 December – Christian wisdom in asking us to renounce ourselves, in reality does not ask for a renunciation but an acquisition. It kindles, in place of human ambitions, a divine ambition. It suggests to us that we put God in the place of our ego: and so raise ourselves from the human level to the divine, entering into fellowship with the Trinity. It is a humility which brings about an infinite dignity. That is why, then, from that summit, the world appears wretched, wealth appears chaff, and positions of eminence appear as sand.

Let us then renounce ourselves in order to be always with God: let us transpose the Eternal into time, make earth Paradise. Then suffering is the raw material of greatness, the Cross a ladder to the Eternal Father.

26 December – Life is a unique opportunity given us for loving. It is a natural instinct to exploit one's neighbour. Let us organise and develop this instinct in a supernatural way, exploiting our brothers. Exploiting one's brother in a Christian way means loving him, serving him to the point of deriving all the merits of that action, its profits, from God: so as to wring from all this God for ourselves; that is eternal life, wealth without end: joy in time and in eternity.

1957

18 February – A person converted to God from a life of sin, after several years of life in a convent, confessed to me her disappointment and her intention to pass on to other experiences, in order to find Christ. I told her that Christ's will is unity: "That all may be one"; and that to separate oneself is equivalent to setting oneself against his Will. She complained of the avarice she had encountered, the rigidity of the written law: and I told her that before God we are not responsible for the ill deeds of others: we are responsible for what we do, each of us, to obey the divine law. The failings of others do not exonerate me from giving love. Christ lives and the Church is holy provided I let him live in me and I become holy. Evils are not eliminated by flying from them but by opposing good to them, making of our persons a barrier of virtue; and the ills of the Church's body are not cured by adding a further ill: that would be a desertion.

26 February – They are right in comparing the cycle of existence to the cycle of the seasons. It is like a tree that grows, flowers, and bears fruit while between its branches the birds build their nests. Then, the bad season comes, trials and storms, and it strips the branches of their foliage and dries them up; until the divine pruner prunes them. He prunes them and reduces the plant to the essential: to a cross.

Life: a growth towards solitude. At the end, you remain alone. *Solus cum sola*. Then your soul converses only with God. To this stupendous result lead disappointments and sufferings, betrayals and deaths.

25 May – The most obvious comparison which occurs to me when I contemplate what I have done is that my life is like a tree in autumn, when it loses its leaves and is left naked. One by one the illusions drop away; politics, literature, friendship, wealth, prestige. . . . But that is a superficial evaluation. As soon as the eye penetrates further than appearances it finds that this detachment from ephemeral values is a liberation. Even seeing one's labours for religion disregarded by religious men is a delicate attention on the part of the Father. He desires absolute love: pure and distinterested love. He desires to be loved for himself. And men too are to be loved for him. Not for ourselves, then, not for human advantages or earthly decorations or institutional laurels. God alone. It is to this that the river of life always bears us, if we do not lose the unique opportunity which it offers for arriving at the estuary. And the opportunity is lost by seeking to halt the flow in quagmires where the gleam of stagnant water can create the illusion which broken glass used to give to primitive peoples to whom it appeared as pearls.

The sole pearl is this love *alone*.

6 October – The one who directs me guides me ever more decisively towards Christ Crucified; he urges me towards the cross and draws me away from the world. The pattern that he indicates for me is Mary, so that the *via crucis*, the way of the Cross, is the *via Mariae*, the way of Mary.

Contemplating existence with the eyes of Mary Desolate how can a man be complacent over something he has written, over some praise he has received, when at our side the Son hangs on his cross.

I must take my stand before Him and therefore before humanity recapitulated in him, in the attitude of Mary, who *'stabat'*, stood, at the foot of the cross, when he was dying and everything was falling in ruins: she stood there, upright, supported by love alone, by which her grief also was mastered: and after he had been taken down, she received her crucified Son on to her knees, holding him, dead, in her arms as she had held him thirty-three years earlier when newly born. Never did she appear such a queen as when she so mastered her suffering in this way. She, a human creature, who holds dead on her lap that Son who was God. She supported herself on that dead one who was Life.

The desolation of the Virgin was the counterpart on the human side (on the part of a woman) of the Son's desolation in the divine when he felt himself abandoned by the Father. The human–divine drama of Mary completed the divine–human drama of Jesus: the single drama of the Redemption; for in that abandonment we, the scattered sons of Adam, were found again.

Meditating on this mystery, on such regality of suffering, on the evening of the First of October, a month sacred to Mary, after prayers, all of a sudden my soul was cleared of human things and persons and in their places Mary entered, together with Jesus, drained of his Blood, and the whole abode of my soul was filled by her figure of suffering and of love. And with her in me I grasped the frivolity of my attachment to transient things. For twenty-four hours. She was there, like an altar holding the victim: *Virgo altare Christi,* the virgin Christ's altar. My soul was her abode, her temple. But at the end of twenty-four hours, sharing in her anguish and love for her brought about a unity between her and my soul and it seemed that she became my soul: she was no longer my guest, but I was her guest, so that I could say: "It is no longer I who live but Mary who lives in me".

Her presence had as it were, virginized my soul, marianized my person. My ego seemed to be dead and in its place Mary was born. So that I no longer felt the need to raise my eyes to the street shrines or to statues of the Madonna; it was enough and it is enough for me to turn the gaze of my soul within myself, to discern in the place of the usual grimy and grotesque idol her who is wholly beautiful, the Mother of the beautiful Love. And even this poor suffering body seems to me to have become a sort of cathedral in which Mary with the dead

Christ summons the Bridegroom and he assembles the Trinity.

Unless I am the most utter scoundrel I must become a Saint: be in harmony with this reality. Had I not decided that this year was to be the year of my sanctification, that is to say, of the enthronement of God in the place of my ego.

25 October – Frivolous as I am, I tremble, I must tremble, at the thought that my person is the abode, must be the abode of the Trinity: must receive the Father, Being; the Son, Reason; the Holy Spirit, Love. For this reason too I rejoice, I must rejoice, that Mary has become the guest of my soul, mistress of my person, Queen and soul of my soul; only she, as daughter, can welcome the Eternal Father; only she, as Mother, can welcome the Eternal Son; only she, as Bride can welcome Eternal Love. But in this way the Blessed Trinity delights to come into this cave, inhabited by animals and to transform it into a temple. Into it the Power of God comes down, the Saviour is born in it, the Paraclete breathes, around Mary. I do not exist: I am lost in her and through her in God: and this is what I wanted.

15 November– I feel that I have arrived at the autumn of life: the last fruits have been gathered and eaten, the last leaves have been blown away by cold gusts of wind. I am well aware of it: my inward youthfulness resists, as if fortified by trials: this lack of affections and satisfactions coming from men has tempered it, sharpened it as it were, made it a prow that advances towards the Mystery; so that the plant seems to gather itself together to bear fruit again in eternity.

I have endeavoured for decades, without growing discouraged and ever starting afresh at the beginning, to give myself to persons and to institutions, to ideals and to services; and it seemed to me that I was giving myself as though consecrating myself without counting the cost, joyfully. Now it seems, as I look back on it, that I sowed failures to reap a harvest of ingratitude, as if persons and things, one after the other, had exploited and deceived me. They have all taken, few or none have given.

I understand, and I am not surprised. The mistake is to look for a return from man, whereas it comes from God. And God has not disappointed me: he feeds my heart daily with a youthful love, one ready to begin again from the start. Have I not written several times that when one serves one's brother one serves the Father? That one loves God by loving one's neighbour?

Experience bears out the lesson, which is this: that things and persons are to be loved not for their own sake and still less for my sake, but for the sake of God. And God gives the hundredfold in this life and beatitude in the next. And that is what God is doing.

The fruit and the leaves fall but from their decayed substance flowers a new Spring. In the solitude which is taking over in preparation for winter God stands out: he is drawing near; and my relationship with him is becoming more intimate and more immediate. To the extent that it loses in the human economy, it is gaining in the divine economy. Creatures detach themselves in order that I may become attached to the Creator. I fail to find love, in order that I may find Love.

The season will come to an end, action will end together with the reactions of men, when at last I will be with God. In him there is no more history: which is a record of time, as it were a list of those who have died. In eternity there is pure life, and it is full because lived in unity with God. And God is beyond time, with its seasons and their fruit and their leaves.

Seen thus existence is a tree that grows towards heaven, to flower in eternity. Seasons and disasters, disappointments and sufferings are the prunings. The tree grows beneath a rain of bitter water (weeping is water and sun), to be cleansed, until it becomes a pure trunk rising from earth to heaven.

Life is only a process of ripening, by means of the purification which suffering brings about in it: when it is ripe, God, who transplants the tree into Paradise, gathers the fruit.

6 December – If physical existence is a combustion let us make of the body a thurible and pour into it without ceasing the incense of our prayer. In this way, looking at it from another viewpoint, there comes about the union of human and divine, of body and spirit; always as a projection of unity, of the God-Man. Every act of charity poured on to those embers will stir up a flame in them; every pain inflicted on us will produce ash, and it will be a consummation like the flame on the altar, if all the love and all the suffering – the suffering become love – are drawn towards where gravity attracts them: to Eternal Love. In this chemistry acts as support to mysticism: and nature's accorded its outlet: its mouth is opened for prayer. Even matter, even cells, are made to return to their Creator.

1958

6 January – How just and wise is the Lord who, in addition to being Father, is Teacher! He has accepted the homage of my writings and takes them at their word. Now he wishes that after having penned them I should live them; and transform into living experience in my flesh and my soul, my teaching on renunciation, silence, incomprehension and suffering. He holds me worthy of suffering: after his own example, he accustoms me to the wages which are now current coin, repaying services with rebuffs, love with abandonment. And so, today, the Eiphany, the Lord appears to me also, in his reality as Redeemer, who redeems with blood: and he grants even my slight suffering its part in the redemption of humanity. So it is that my suffering is not wasted nor rejected. If the gratitude of mortals is lacking, there is the gratitude of the Creator. Now indeed, and not when I was writing books, I am taking part in a cosmic work, at the level of Christ: now that I am refuse, humanly speaking, Christ with suffering supernaturally associates me with his redemptive dignity. It appears to be a collapse and it is a flight upwards.

26 February – The pruning continues. Friendships, hopes, joys, have been cut away. As a writer I am not read; as a Catholic I am not welcomed; as a politician I am disregarded. I had bound myself to a religious family and found joy in communion in Christ and in a common life in Mary. My dillettantism and my pretensions, my judgement and my inability to obey have made the connection impossible for me and in any case it was of itself almost severed; maintained only by slender threads. I would be inclined to level reproaches of inconsistency and ingratitude, but who will assure me that they would not arise from wounded self-love and would not damage charity? Better to retreat into silence; the silence of winter, in which, like a bare plant, existence stretches out lean arms towards heaven and no longer has anything but Christ. All this love given is like all the sun of the summer that is over, the warmth of which has been banished by this cold that numbs my hands and feet, my heart and my mind. I would like to cry out: My God, my God, why have you forsaken me? – but I am afraid of mouthing rhetoric, I regard myself as an actor. And then. . . . And then, I am aware of the inflow into my spirit of a fine and serene joy, as if from a deep peace; and it is like the perfume of lilies and roses, flowering in a sunken garden, and its name is Mary. She is there: and at once this meditation on winter and solitude appears as mere literature to me; for, in spite of everything, when she is there, poetry is accompanied by youthfulness and nostalgia by peace. I will love more than before: but without interfering, in silence, not furthering my own self but furthering God – Holy Love.

1 May – The key to life (relations with God and with our neighbours) bears the name 'love' and to love is to serve. It is all there. Simple, as the things of God are.

Before God one stands as before the Creator, the Almighty, the Judge, even if he is Love and the Father and makes us one with him. The liturgy with which we honour him is service; and likewise the works by which we live, which are to be done in order to love him and serve him in this life.

Before man, before each man as superior (St. Vincent used to say: a master), the lower his social position, the higher one considers him. This reality simplifies human relationships enormously: I am a servant, the other is a master. I serve for love of God, because in serving the other I serve (i.e. I love) God; the other bestows on me the gift of allowing me to reach, by passing through him, the King of Kings; he allows me to love, in him my brother, God the Father. As a result of this, in addition to the worth deriving from creation and redemption, of which he is the object, my brother is for me the practical equivalent of Christ: he is the image of God and I must treat him as I would treat Jesus. In reality when dealing with my neighour, I enter definitively into relationship with God.

But if this is so, it is absurd and useless to complain if I am not loved and therefore served by other men. I have the right to serve them, not to be served. Therefore if my dedication meets with ingratitude, incomprehension and abandonment on the part of others, I must not grieve on my own account; if at all, on their account. My duty is to give, not to receive. "In love, what counts is to love"; "to love" (active), not "to be loved" (passive).

This activity, this giving, this service, is the real stuff of life, and of a life which does not disappoint and such service wins eternal life.

In dark hours, when this clarity is obscured, I must see myself as being like Christ on the Cross, scorned, wounded, abandoned, Universally abandoned. But, it was by this that he accomplished the Redemption and rose again and has been loved for twenty centuries by the flower of humanity: by the martyrs, who offer him their blood, by the apostles, who give him their labours: by the vigins, who for his sake renounce everything else; by parents, who for his sake brave the adventure of the family.

And then, precisely, when the desolation caused by desertion and the anguish arising from my failures comes hurtling down upon me like a hurricane, then precisely I attain the highest dignity in the closest conformity with the Abandoned one: precisely then do I serve, serve all the more the cause of the Church, of redemption, of my own eternal happiness.

When I remain alone, in this desolation, if it is made fruitful by distinterested and unrequited service, then I am one with the Blessed Trinity, with Mary, Virgin and Mother, with the Blessed in heaven and with souls on earth that love. I enjoy the company of none of them: but I am in unity and solidarity with all of them, in that total communion which is the Church.

And so I must not look for gratitude or services from others: I have no right to that. If in serving my neighbour I serve God through him, I should look for gratitude, if at all, from God. And this means, I look for everything from God, nothing from men; only, I look for it not as gratitude (poor me! all that I have and all that I give is his) but as a gift, even if he loves to give it as recompense or reward to the one who serves him.

Therefore if in human relationships someone has the right to be disappointed, it is not I but my brother, whoever he may be, because he indeed has the right to be served; and if I do not serve him he has the right to be disappointed and to complain about me, and God with him.

One acquits oneself of one's divine and human task of contributing to the Passion of Christ, by suffering, and not by making others suffer. And this suffering also, because of the ingratitude or the offences of one's brother, becomes, in the economy of the divine justice and charity, a service. A serving of God in one's neighbour. The evil that comes to us then from our brother becomes a good in the service of our brother. In serving, everything is turned into good.

To serve is to reign: this is the revolution of the Cross.

18 May – Faced with the problems of life I find that I propose various solutions in accordance with the point of view from which I approach them. If I start from love, I tackle the problem in one way; if I start from self–interest in another way. Likewise if I start from laziness, from selfishness, from vanity. . . . And they will be wrong or inadequate solutions: for, in every case, and for every case, I avoid making a mistake only if I start from charity: if I see men and things with the heart of Christ, with the eyes of Mary: then I am seeing them in the light of the Holy Spirit. And he is Love.

20 June – With the passage of the years poetry, pine grove of the spring, withers: the enhantment of woman, morning flower, is quenched; the attraction of colours and of nature, of art and of technology is lessened. Ever more, amidst this stripping of petals and leaves, amidst dry branches on the barren plain, there arises, alone but sufficient, the poetry of the Virgin: Mary rises up, filling all the empty spaces, filling the darkness with light, intoning the hymn of creation: she is the whole of Beauty, unfading poetry. As soon as her Name flowers in the desert, everything is coloured with youthfulness.

I need everyone and no-one. God alone: I only need God. Without food I cannot live, without air I suffocate, without clothes I freeze, without friendship I am saddened. Joy comes from the members of my family, and from my companions; utility comes from my rivals and my enemies, since by obliging me to forgive them they ask for love: and to love is joy. And nonetheless, I can do without everything and everyone, I can even die after suffering agonies. But if God is there, in him everything is nothing; nothing is for him everything. He makes death the gate to life, abandonment an epiphany: through him suffering is access to the Wound in which Paradise is found. How much good my parents and my brothers, my wife and children, my relations and benefactors have done me from my infancy up to the present moment: and nonetheless, when I lose them I find them again in God. If I lose God I lose all of them together with myself. They are all useful: God alone is necessary. Only with him I have with me everyone, from eternity.

23 June – Observing, with a pang, this falling of leaves (illusions of fame and power and friendship) from the tree of my life, in this autumn turned to winter, I am still better aware that the ever deeper and more impenetrable solitude by which I am surrounded is brought about for a more intense loving intercourse with God: the soul finds time and leisure at last for talking with the Bridegroom. They call this solitude an approach to death: and it is an approach to life. Now finally I can let my soul listen to the Holy spirit, live with the angels and the blessed, unite myself with Christ and with God. And God is life. Previously too many distractions and interruptions prevented the passage of God's spirit, which is Life: now, gradually, union is becoming constant. I am learning and preparing the life of Paradise.

I have always wanted to reach God because I have always been hungry for life: but even while drawing near to him, I used to interpose, like valves, my studies, my friendships, my habits; and often I took my ease in them: I stopped at creatures and phantasms: I sacrificed the essential to the inessential, the divine to the human.

Now the passage is clear: I and God. I to be lost in God. I, who am not, to be lost in God, who is. I must not revert to cluttering up that space again with the debris of disappointments and complaints, of resentments and envies. . . . Now I have God alone: the whole of God: what else can be of any use to me?

1 September – If the summit of religion consists in service, it is useless, a waste of time and of peace, to stay delving into one's self in quest of injured rights and slights received. If religion is, practically speaking, service, there are not any rights to be injured. There are only duties to be performed: and rather we should complain when we stop ourselves from loving God by serving our brothers.

Seen this way, every supposed curtailment of rights or disregard of titles would be seen as a confirmation or an approval, so that the man who disregards or offends us is co-operating with us, imbuing our day with the flavour and the colour of the Blood of Christ Crucified. Then when we seem to be abandoned, we are with him on the Cross, we are abandoned with him: we are the one Christ crying out.

2 September – If you make yourself nothing, God fills you with himself. If you put yourself on the floor of humility, you put yourself on the level of contentment, where the problem is solved: there you do not look for wealth, since you love poverty, and so you set yourself free from the economic stimulus which causes humanity such feverish suffering: there, insults and misunderstandings become virtues for you and you divest your spirit of the hair shirt of wounded pride: there, you have no grounds for setting yourself above anyone and you offer to charity, which is life, the whole space to

62

circulate, you find once again the human family and the divine Trinity, you rediscover the Church and you live as a fellow citizen of the Saints.

You are in humility, in simplicity, at ease and above all in liberty. You make yourself the imitator of Mary, whose humility gave its consent to the Incarnation: and you too incarnate God for men, in a certain way.

9 September – These abandonments by men throw open the desert of God: daily humiliations till it. The only tree of life which flourishes there, amidst the desolate vastness, is the trunk of the Cross. At its foot appears Mary. And Calvary is repeated, and you are admitted to it, as spectator and as actor, in order that you may share in the salvific sacrifice: and this is an act of association with the divine, which is certainly worth more than the frenzy of traffic amidst shouting and immodest fashions.

The Cross; meeting-place for God, who becomes man, to redeem and for man who becomes God, if he is redeemed.

Priesthood, virginity and matrimony are the three sides of an isosceles triangle: two of them stretch up towards heaven converging on God and meeting in him, the third, which extends along the earth and begets priests and virgins, through them communicates with heaven. The first two bring graces from God; the third incarnates them in humanity and reciprocally gathers from humanity the prayers which by those two paths it causes to mount to heaven. A triad which intermingles the divine in the human and the human in the divine. If love circulates between them they are three and they are one: they are God's viaduct, to bring about the incarnation of the son. At the centre of the triangle is Mary, Mother of Christ, the Eternal Priest, herself a Virgin and Bride.

1 October – The wisdom of Christ Crucified prescribes detachment from human affections and achievements: it teaches liberation. And in order that this may not become selfishness it teaches at the same time love, which is service of human beings.

If such detachment is not accepted as a norm of wisdom it will be accepted as a result of violence; for, bit by bit, men and things will desert us (we shall say in bewilderment that they are betraying us). Growth in years becomes growth in solitude, in abandonment. Christ mounted the Cross, after serving the Father in heaven and men on earth, to contemplate in anguish the scattering of his disciples on earth and abandonment by the Father in heaven. It is the logic of the Redemption. The man who accustoms himself to abandonment, who of his own accord effects detachment in himself, need have no fears; the man who does not do that, laments, as if lost in an icy polar region.

5 October – When certain saints are mentioned to me or when I think of them, they come running to my side as members of my family, even though coming from a distance of centuries; a Paul, an Augustine, an Agnes. . . . I know almost nothing about her: and yet I am at home with her: mother, teacher, sister . . . and Catherine, Clare, Bernard, Teresa, Vincent and the little Thérèse . . . familiar faces, each with the light which is his or her own. And then, solitude is explained all the better: it is a return to our family begun here below, where with Father and Mother and the one Brother, in the warmth of the Holy Spirit, are all these writers and doctors and confessors and martyrs, all these virgins consecrated to God, and housewives and children, with a cloud of angels: it is a celebration. Each one of them makes everyone love giving particular joy to Mary who is Love.

Today's decision at the feet of Saint Mary Magdalen: *silence and nothingness*. Silence in regard to the exterior, becoming nothing in regard to the interior: the void which God will fill.

And in fact, immediately after, that joy which is the atmosphere of the divine returned.

11 November – How can one get bored in life if the City of God is there to be built up? How can one suffer from desolation if one can live in communion with God? How can one feel oneself alone, if in solitude above all one can converse with God? The Word demands Silence.

1959

17 January – Seen in God this process which we call growing old is a progress towards God, a drawing near home: the return journey, which approaches the goal.

20 January – The laborious but continual detaching of oneself from human appearances, this immersion of oneself in God, is at the present moment an act of marianization; one comes to identify oneself gradually with God by identifying oneself, or to the extent to which one identifies oneself, with Mary: for to become Mary is to become Jesus. It is she who upholds and purifies, and in every shadow and after every fall she imparts new light to the eyes and restores one's strength: she is guide and teacher, mother and Queen: the Lady who sets free, re-making us continually as sons of God in order that without stopping on the way we may travel towards the Father. She is the *Janua Coeli*, the Gate of Heaven, and we go to God, who is the soul's heaven, by her. To martyrdom and to sacrifice, which may be the cost, Mary adds the smile of poetry and the lights of hope, by which beatitude in God is anticipated.

27 January – How can one become bored with life if the *City of God* is there to be built up? How can one have any dread of old age if it is a growth towards heaven, a continual progress towards the solution? And the solution is joy. Eternity: Life.

17 February – Today you have acknowledged (and you could have done so with less fuss) that you are a nuisance to a charitable undertaking which is dear to you. You have sacrificed yourself for it: but in the end your person and your way of seeing things are found to be a nuisance. Perhaps this too is an act of love, after you have found by experience that not even humbling yourself is any use now, not even service. God has no need of you for his works: perhaps you serve more in this way, by disappearing.

18 February – I too say, and so many times, that it must no longer be I who am but Christ who is in me: he must be I. I say too that I must be a void to be filled by God, a nothing in order to offer myself to the All. But then, I spend a large part of the day curled up in my own self, talking banalities and practising the deceits of the world; thus I am in myself, that is, nothing, in emptiness. Because I must busy myself for a large part of the day with earthly things, I make my soul live on a level that is half, if not wholly, subterranean.

And instead I ought to fill myself with God, even when I am attending to the things of the world: allow Christ to live, always, to the very last minute of the 24 hours, whatever I may be doing: I should be, in every thought and relationship, impregnated with the divine; so that the divine becomes my nature and I act as an expression of Christ, with the heart of his Mother, with the standards of the Church.

Then everything is simplified: fears vanish, suffering takes on a meaning; nature becomes a temple; the created being leads me to its Creator. There is no need for you to be anxious or to get angry with men, since you love them; and in this way, in addition to everything else, you neutralise them in regard to yourself and endow them with value in regard to God.

3 May – Betrayals, falls, disappointments . . . hurricanes, as it were, which sweep away edifices built up with silent care, in the deep nights of idolatrous worship of one's own self. These cataracts which humiliations are, cause anguish and yet they cleanse. They are purifying waters which sweep away the castles of pride and the showcases of vanity. They clear a space for sight and for action, uncovering the reality of the relationship which eludes me: I, nothing – God, all. They are accordingly a growth in the vision of God, an increase of his presence, a richer phase of his action. Grace establishes itself on the ground that has been cleansed and cleared: true life grows.

A new vision comes of it, almost scientifically, with the science of God – clear vision, making possible the elimination of suffering from disappointments, ingratitude and slights. These were present because in my neighbour I saw myself: always myself. Now in my brother Christ is seen once again: even in the depraved brother: for Christ came for sinners. And the one thing that matters is to also love the depraved for love of him: to love him also in the depraved; so that life is transformed only into love of God. As I love him amidst labours, so I love him amidst insults; the essential thing is not to let oneself be separated from him by paper screens, gaseous screens, of rancour and vanity.

5 July – Socially, religion is only service. Service is the highest dignity of man: a ladder for mounting to God.

For to serve is to love in *deed,* as Christ loved us, giving us all, without asking for anything. When one begins to claim a return, one descends from the divine to the subhuman.

Between two souls in love with God, conversation is necessarily, a conversation of love, in which the greatest words of love are exchanged: one says: Jesus; the other replies: Mary. And so, their love is the Holy Spirit.

10 July – The most moving feature of Mary's love for us is that she allows us to love her; to love her as Mary, as the Love of all: then love makes her Queen, Teacher, Mistress, Mother. Let that which will fall in life, fall: nothing can take us away from loving Mary. And this gives joy, stirs up poetry, creates beauty, opens paradise. . . . (You touch on the subject of Mary and you never come to an end of singing her praises: Mary is loved by singing, because Mary is Love).

31 August – On the 22nd of this month I consecrated myself to the Immaculate Heart of Mary together with thousands of my brothers and sisters. And, if I am consecrated, I belong to Mary, as her possession, her creature. Like the objects of devotion to her. I am in her heart, like the *ex-voto* offerings in her shrines, like the sacred images, vestments, and altars in the chapels dedicated to her. Now indeed she is for me Sovereign, Mistress, Teacher, Mother . . . but my abode is her heart, that heart in which love for God first found a lodging, making her a Handmaid, from which there was formed the Blood of the Redeemer, and from which the *Magnificat* burst forth. . . . To belong in this way to Mary: a gift that never ceases to astound me and to bind me to her when it comes to me.

1960

1 January – God, the Blessed Trinity, Mary: my Love, fruit of your Love. You have given me life, you have given me the Redemption; now, grant me further time to avail myself of it: to make of 1960, all of it, or some part of it, it does not matter, a further opportunity for loving you, by loving and living, your Love. For this Lord, grant me to be Mary, she who is full of God and bestows Jesus; so that every instant, every occupation, every word – even the most remote from the things of

God, may be a movement towards you and everything may be directed to the Eternal, and the twenty-four hours of every day may be the means and the ever-varying modes of honouring you: life as liturgy. And in this way, sorrow becomes love, suffering purifies, labour is prayer. And then, Lord, again, thank you, thank you for having given us Mary, Mother, Teacher, Queen, Our Lady.

2 January – As gradually the years mount up, old people, in many cases, return to religion, or become more religious. This development is called involution; this progress, regression and senility. And instead it is an instinctive warning of the proximity of God and of judgment: the proximity, better still, of home.

When the leaves have fallen from the tree, the trunk opens its branches to heaven; it is rained upon, enveloped in mist, struck by lightning; but it looks upwards, no longer deceived by foliage: no longer deceived by what passes. It now accustoms itself to, has a foretaste of, what endures.

My person, Mary's abode, situated in her will, gathers itself together, more and more, into the abode of Eternal Love, whose masterpiece is the Mother.

3 January – The Name of Jesus. . . . It is enough to call it to mind to scatter phantasms, to banish fear, to bring love and joy into the aridity of one's affections, kindling the constellations of hope in the Eternal even over the ploughed land of a monotonous chronicle of adulteries and impurities, each one more imbecile than the one before: all of them, challenges to misfortune and stormy provocations.

Jesus: he is strength, and sorrow suffered in silence, and the certainty of resurrection, and he is victory over death; he is the sacrifice of self to one's brother and for one's brother, to the Father.

Jesus: the destroyer of evil (and hypocrisy, calculation, exploitation is what is evil) the Lord of time.

He would have us all one: all Jesus. And this is the greatest gift of his love; making us all himself.

For this we entrust ourselves to Mary, handmaid of the Lord, in order to give the world to Jesus. She continues to cultivate Jesus in us, until our ego has been broken down and it is no longer we individually who live but Christ who lives in us.

4 January – When what can be plumbed has been plumbed, one reaches in the end deadlock: the obstacle which prevents the life of God from passing into us. The hard, earthy, bestial, obstacle is the ego, before which, albeit in secret, we are prostrate in adoration.

The conflict, it is clear, is not only between the World, the Flesh, Money and Vice on the one hand, and God on the other: the conflict is essentially between God and the ego, since this latter is made up of Avarice, Lust, Ambition. . . .

The saint is the man who definitively, or at least at decisive moments, expels the ego, the rubbish cluttering up the room. The saint creates emptiness in himself by removing that muddy litter, and so he makes room for God.

Let us then cease to be concerned about ourselves: let us entrust our destiny to God.

5 January – Today is the feast of a Virgin. . . the Church opposes virginity to depravity, which remains and over-flows in the form of lust through the agency of prostitutes: she corrects Eve with Mary. And since today Eve is dominant, she brings in the age of Mary, who shows herself also in the persons of virgins: and these, against the din of lust and the pretensions of culture, live a spiritual maternity, which saves religion in the world: Mary who never ceases to give Jesus to men.

6 January – The Apparition of Jesus: but in the hands of Mary. This is today's feast. And as such it has been renewed for us too, to whom has been given the gift of seeing Jesus and the Church again as it were in their infancy, because it was Mary, the humility, purity and virginal feminity that reverses Eve, who showed him to the world. And this seems to me to be the reality of this Marian age, which awaits a new spring in the Church, at an epoch in which, with Satan at large in the world, as Catherine Emmerich saw, only the Blessed Virgin can trample on his neck.

10 January – If the family became aware of its sacrament and developed it . . . that is, if in addition to carrying out its functions in regard to birth, work, illness and care, entertainment and anxieties, it fulfilled also its sacramental role as the organ for transmitting divine life, in addition to physical life, and as copy of the household of Nazareth, so that the father was Christ and the Mother the Church and the child was Christ-Church; if it were in the world as a representative of the Eternal, as the Church giving Christ to men and making of its fellowship a participation in the Trinitarian fellowship of God in heaven, realising unity in trinity (father, mother, child = a single heart and a single soul) then its course on earth would be a repetition of Calvary, that is, it would bring forth redemption and resurrection.

11 January – Today's martyr★ reminds me that I must be ready to give my life for the Lord. There are periods and places in which the offering of one's blood is not customary: the same value attaches to an offering which is no less effective: the offering of mind and heart, to the Church and for the Church. It is made into the hands of Superiors who, through the Hierarchy, go back to the Pope and through him to God. For my part there could

---

★ St. Hyginus, Pope and Martyr: d. 142: the author's patron saint.

not be any more serious renunciation. And that must be so. When in a matter which demands much of me, I relinquish my own judgement for that of my Superiors, that is to say of God, I have given my intellectual and moral life: I have accomplished the martyrdom of mind and will.

But then I find that I have relinquished the human and found the divine: and in the place of the self I find God.

13 January – If the greatest gift made to us by God is freedom, the greatest offering that we can make to him is freedom; and this then is the greatest free act.

On the other hand, this renunciation amounts to substituting for one's own will the Will of God: that is to say, becoming him by participating in his will: and he is eternal freedom.

That is, the renunciation is only apparent; for in reality it consists in anchoring one's own heart and will in the Blessed Trinity: for the purpose of fortifying it and insuring it against the changes of the human will, comparable to those of the sea's billows.

14 January – The marian operation in progress is a counter-attack by the Blessed Virgin against the rebel Angel, who rages above all in sexual disorder.

It is an operation which leads us to work for the building of a new city, a City of God, which in its first phase is a City of Mary (Mariapolis), it's constitutionally organized so that in it God reigns and Our Lady governs.

16 January – The thought, form and remembrance of Mary fill the soul with light, like a deep emerald pool. It is a fact, the soul is kneaded into her: it is marianized; it becomes her. As Daughter she bears the Father; and as Mother she brings the Son; and as Bride, she summons the Holy Spirit. Virgin and Mother, she awakes the Church. Her chaste hands bear the sacraments, as jewels; her daughterhood wrests love from the Trinity and, with love, wisdom, and she joins the two qualities with purity. Mother of graces, she sprinkles the path of life with joys, gives life to hope, tends piety, makes of existence an act of love, in which she changes the sufferings into a holocaust. Mary is poetry: to be her, to be full of her, is to be full of God; and then one lives in fellowship with the Trinity, and she is the lady of the house.

17 January – On investigation, beneath the silences and the reserve of the saints, one finds that the flame of their zeal, the secret of their self-giving, the inward love that drove them on and held them up, was Mary: one finds that their charity and as it were the light of their genius were in proportion to their love for Mary. On this they drew continually, again and again returning to silence from activity and from speaking: for that love was a flight which took them to God and God then gave them back to men.

The secret love of the Church is Mary: the perennial renewal of its virginity is inspired by Mary and is nourished by the graces that are transmitted by her.

Sometimes the saints do not speak much about her because they guard her name and her form in the depths of their soul, as if to shield her immaculateness from the incomprehension with which the surrounding world meets it in its depravity.

18 January – I am on the ridge of a crisis; on either side there gapes an abyss; one of light, the other of dizziness.

For years I have worked to defend and exalt the Church: and now, as a result, my name no longer appears in the newspapers. I am no longer invited to congresses. . . . It ought to discourage me, like a blast of frozen air from the pole of death: oblivion and ingratitude.

And instead, when I think it over carefully, here too the jealous God is sweeping away every human attraction and support: and He is ensuring that my work is done solely for him, in total disinterestedness, and for that very reason is capable of greater beauty and greatness.

Solus cum sola (Alone with the alone): I must see here his jealous love for my soul and stand fast in universal solitude.

24 January – Every time one opens a newspaper one reads reports and reflections on political disagreements, which are brought about by conflicts in economics and by various ambitions. . . . And one learns of speeches and undertakings to restore order and re-establish unity, but with scant success. I am inclined to think that what is wanted is a charge of love, in the world in which selfishness carries all before it: love would create the 'new man' afresh in all, would put Christ in all: and Christ is one; and politics would become the construction of the City of God. In all this, in fact, is the love of God carried to contempt of self. In the other approach there is the love of self pushed to contempt of God.

How fresh is this emphasis of St. Augustine's.

26 January – The Lord is drawing me close to himself – he is uniting me to himself in order to transform me into himself, by means of that pedagogy, I would almost say that chemistry, which suffering is: the darkness of suffering. When I think it over, all at once it appears to me with the clarity of a flame, in the night: the very fuel of his Passion, in the Garden of Olives and on the summit of Calvary. Is the Cross approaching?

Be it so, provided that Mary is at its side, and it is no longer I who live but Jesus who lives in me, so that I can cry out, after the abandonment, after the *Eloi, Eloi,* "Into thy hands Father, I commend my spirit".

28 January – Yesterday evening I found myself in the aridity of a desert without a blade of grass: raging with thirst. I was suffering universal abandonment: I had no awareness of God, Love, and I had no love for men. But I understood why the Saints had chosen not joy but suffering, in abandonment, like Christ on the Cross. I understood why Christ had asked us to take up his Cross and having left everything, to follow him. . . .

In that solitude, as if my spirit had been quenched, I fell asleep.

And this morning, a popular hymn to Our Lady – such a sweet one! burst from my lips, and from her, love has returned like the blue of morning and the water of a spring. As from the *humus* (soil) that is trodden down, turned over, made sour by chemical substances, there springs up a flower, from desolation there springs up incarnate Love, Mary. Mary who gives us Incarnate Love. . . .

Is Mary then the secret for bringing love out of suffering?

30 January – Mary is the Virgin who makes of her person a lamp lighted to the glory of God, and of her existence an uninterrupted *Magnificat,* a whole hymn and a programme.

It is noteworthy that we say 'Mary' without prefixing any title: her royalty lies in this simplicity; powerful as a queen, enlightened as a teacher, venerated as a mother, nonetheless she lets herself be designated by a name conveying familiarity and she succeeds in preserving amidst this sisterly service, the dignity of Mother of God, Our Lady and Sovereign.

But how splendid life is when the name of Mary is lighted up at the head of the stairs, like a light! Should we not thank God indeed for having granted us the smiling and life-giving company of our Mother for our return to our Father?

2 February – For her purification Mary presented herself to the priest: but it was a purification accomplished not undergone: active, not passive. It was she who was purifying the temple, the priesthood, the world, for which she had borne the Son. And her task, through the Church, by the Church, in the Church, by way of the real priesthood and by way of the royal priesthood, is to purify souls: to restore virginal purity to a world defiled by senile wantonness.

She renews virginity and thus she rejuvenates. And she does this also and most usually by means of women who have resolved to imitate her, purifying themselves in order to purify others.

Spring garden, early morning air, clear sky, like a morning vesture for God's majesty, you are all this, Mary, our poetry, our love, you who enamour us with Eternity.

7 February – I spend whole hours contemplating the faces of human beings and I do not dare to lift my face to Christ Crucified. The former leave me with foolish fancies, a double-faced game; the latter forces truth and reality upon me, brings me up against the vision of eternal things – immeasurable things, and of my own paltriness, shrinking away and preferring to lurk like a farmyard animal in search of a momentary titbit. And so it is that when he is seen human features also appear in their correct proportions and position, so that they no longer deceive or disappoint. To contemplate Christ Crucified is to acquire a divine transparency in one's judgement of human affairs: in order to direct human affairs then, in that light, to the eternal destinations. This is the vision of Eternity.

9 February – The time lost in thinking about the self is indeed time lost: because the self of itself is nothing. God is all: time lived to the full is that which is spent in thinking of God: that is where life is.

How many souls waste their existence by letting it

whirl round and round in that void, that ditch, which opens on to the nothingness of Death!

11 February – Every now and then a plunge. A plunge into a black whirlpool in which nothing is seen, no voice is heard, any longer, and one is left desperately, desolately alone.

I know that those plunges are the meetings of great love with Jesus Forsaken on the Cross: and they should bring me joys: but what usually happens is that I focus what is left of my sight to see myself and to see other men who ought to keep me company; and I do not turn to Christ Crucified, who at my side continues to shed his Blood. And I think that I lack this vision because I do not turn to Mary, who *stabat iuxta crucem* (stood by the Cross) mourning, but alive, with her heart open to the suffering of humanity taken up into the agony of her Son. I have this sure passage to the Eternal which is the Immaculate Heart of Mary: and I do not use it. I am not to be pitied but to be laughed at.

17 February – In the lobbies of the Chamber each deputy I meet relates misfortunes, and brings to light degrading facts. The press denounces corruption, lays bare scandals.

The result of speeches and reading is the realisation that the dialectic of good and evil, even in the political sphere, or, rather, in it especially, confronts one with the dilemma: either to become a saint or to shoot oneself. Two ways of liberation from evil, the outcome of social and spiritual disintegration: only the choice between the two is extremely obvious. One is Life – true liberation; the other is Death – final slavery.

But, although convinced of these truths, as men grow older with the passage of the years, they find toil increasing, irritations multiplying, solitude spreading like a desert, which as night falls, sees the last rare human shadows disappear. Love also sets, like a sun, amidst clouds and the twigs of bare branches.

What does this mean? It means that the Lord creates silence round man, so that he can converse with him in peace and in depth: in order to have him, finally, wholly for himself, he who is the jealous God who would have the soul wholly for himself and, therefore, wholly for immortality.

Solitude therefore is to be seen as an invitation to recollect oneself more seriously and continually in the presence of the Eternal and to give value to the remnant of one's days by occupying one's mind in a higher contemplation with something better than electric domestic appliances, the day's news and noise.

What is this but a paternal intervention on the part of Christ the Teacher, to induce us to translate into our lives his teachings on the fleeting nature of human affections, on the unreliability of earthly constructions. Everything crumbles, only God remains.

To contemplate and to love: to contemplate Love in order to burn away this remnant of life like a solitary flame of love, in silence.

19 February – The Lord has granted it to me to serve him from the lay sector, that is, from below: from the earth *(humi)*, in humility; so that my work will be both a service rendered on my knees, to the Church, and a service rendered as minister in serving others. And this for me is part of my marian vocation, which would have me be a humble figure – the least one – but a real figure of the *Ancilla Domini* (the Handmaid of the Lord). She who, without being a priest, in the lay state, from below, prepared for and served the Priest.

I do not know if, as a layman, any greater mansion could have been accorded me.

25 February – In regard to the world and to men, rather than speak of disappointments they bring us with the passage of the years, it would be more appropriate to speak of clarifications: in fact piece by piece they pull down the castle of idols which we make for ourselves as a hiding place, to avoid contemplating the face of reality; And reality is God: all the rest is illusion. *Deus meus et omnia* (My God and my all). In God is all: outside of him is nothingness, even if clad in bubbles of air.

Mary saw and accepted this reality. When in their village even his relatives set themselves against Jesus, and He was opposed also by the scribes, the persons of consequence and the priests, she did not speak of disappointments; she possessed the reality called Jesus. Rather the world sought to deprive her of it, to erect before her eyes and those of all others the sham wall of sophistries and illusions, behind which it was allowed to cultivate death.

27 February – If we put Mary in the midst of us, human creatures who have come together to work and perhaps play; if we put the Blessed Virgin in our hearts and as a guard on our lips, there is no danger that conversation will degenerate, that a meal will be the occasion of trivialities, that over the smile on people's faces, over the features of the soul, there will trickle the pretentious defilement of vulgarity. Without Mary a meeting of men and women becomes an exchange of impurities, as it were a throwing of slops in one another's faces: and the level of existence sinks to the plane of the dunghill.

Even on the top of this, however, if you bring in Mary at the summit of your thoughts, the spirit revives, like an eagle and soars up to the clear blue: in health the spirit regains poetry and regains beauty above the mud.

29 February – God came down among men in Jesus. Men have gone up to God, in Mary. Jesus and Mary: the double track on which our existence runs, on the journey from earth to heaven, from the human to the divine, from death to Life.

Jesus, Glory of the Trinity, Mary, glory of humanity. Christ is the junction where men connect with God: Mary the Mother and God the Father put him there.

5 March – Christ was charity, charity personified, no less when he cried "Race of vipers! whitened sepulchres!" than when he groaned "Father, forgive them for they know not what they do".

17 March – I have been far from home and, drawn into the vortex of public engagements, I relegated the love of God and of the Mother of God to the fringe: and it was as if I had put out the light. Darkness came down on the road and rain fell: and anger and wrath sprang up like tangled brambles. The Mother was not there, and she did not switch on the light, she did not open the way to the Blessed Trinity, she did not escort the procession of the Saints. . . . All at once I noticed my blindness and called out: Mary! And lo and behold a smile came back to my entangled and dripping soul, a patch of blue sky appeared, light returned. I could not see Mary, I could not see even Jesus in heaven, in my heart and in me, in my brothers: and therefore I could no longer see any brothers: I had entered the net of death.

21 March – The difficulties of life in the Church, the conflicts and at times the delays in the expansion of Christianity do not come so much from non-Christians as from Christians who are engrossed in the worship of money: the enemy is in the last resort Mammon. And sanctity is in the end, and in the beginning, liberation from the shackles of money. As with the Pharisees in the time of Jesus, the exploitation which paralyses religion is carried on beneath the sacred banners, by false Christians who want to defend privileges and accumulate capital. And the poor, often mistake this semblance of sacred things, this cloaking of unwholesome things, for true religion. If the spirit of Mammon takes possession of the spirit of Christian individuals and groups it immobilises their feelings and turns their faith to stone: instead of a living church one has a sarcophagus.

Truly the most arduous part of the effort to attain sanctity consists in freeing oneself from this servitude.

7 April – In the end, it is clear that, in spite of the passage of time, I am still a poet. But it is clear also that in spite of contaminations this poetry has remained: Mary.

How could I have lived, how could I live without her?

It is Mary the Mother of God who continually gives birth to Jesus in me: and Jesus is life, strength and beauty. He is Love.

14 April – God comes down into me by way of bread: I go up to him by way of my brother.

17 April – If our life must be conformed with that of Christ, this applies also to the resurrection. One dies for sin, one rises again for grace. By this we know that we pass from death to life: if we love our brethren. The man who loves, lives God, and God is life.

This reality, at communion this morning, came home to me in the light of the Christmas scene. My person, through the corrosion of anger, pride, vanity and mutability is a gaping manger – come to it Mary, with Joseph, and give birth to Jesus in it – and then it becomes a temple, more sacred than a cathedral.

It seems to me that my heavenly Mother brought me contentment (can she ever fail to bring us contentment?): and this body of mine, worn out as it is and borne up by a soul equally tattered, as a sanctuary: Mary's abode, a tabernacle for Christ, a dwelling for Joseph and for all the saints; Martyrs, Doctors, Virgins, Confessors. . . . Humanly speaking I have failed: supernaturally I am consecrated to Mary, have become a member of Christ's family, I have risen to a celestial dignity: the kindred of the Creator.

19 April – Resurrection for man is conversion: and that means death to sin and ignorance, and resurrection into Truth and Light. Conversion, which ought to be repeated every day, means the crucifixion of the old man and the birth of the new man: a victory over senescence which sinks into death.

22 April – Weariness increases, irritations multiply, solitude grows more intense, like a sun between clouds and the twigs of naked trees. Now what is this but an invitation to recollect oneself more seriously and continually in the presence of God, to give the rest of one's life some value in a more serious service, with fewer distractions? What is this but a fatherly intervention on the part of Christ the Teacher persuading us to translate into action the teachings given us in regard to the fleeting nature of human affections? Everything collapses, only God remains. To love is to serve, not to be served, it is giving not receiving. The recompense is given by God: the fruit is his love.

23 April – Illness, lived in love, produces a spiritual health, which communicated to the mystical body, repays with treasures of holiness, gifts of soups and medicines. In the sick, Christ repays as only he knows how, giving the Infinite for a glass of water.

1 May – The saint after all is nothing else but a man in love: in love with the Godhead reflected and brought close to Mary. The saint is one in love with Our Lady and his love consists precisely in becoming one with her: losing himself in her, making her life his own. Thereby he makes her humility, purity and service of God his own to the point that he makes of his soul a simple *Ancilla Domini* (Handmaid of the Lord) and thus he makes himself capable of 'giving birth' to Christ for humanity.

The saint, man or woman, is a copy of Mary. When one explores the depths of his mystery, one finds this enamouring and fascinating ideal which is the Virgin Mother: it is always Mary who thus arouses love for Jesus.

9 May – Asceticism gives earth the title of vale of tears, place of exile and makes life a pilgrimage of foreigners in a strange land. That is true, but only up to a certain point. For on to this region amidst the planets, this tiny atom amidst the constellations, Mary came, Christ was born, the saints lived; and the Church is here and the churches are here and in them lives the Eucharist and from them issues charity.

On these clods of earth the Saints have brought holiness to flower; doctors, their teaching; virgins, their virginity; upright layfolk, their uprightness. And so it is an exile, but lived in the company of the Son of God and of Mary his Mother, with the assistance of the apostles and the confessors; lived in fellowship with the angels and the blessed. And there is love amongst the pilgrims: and the love is God in them; and where God is, there is no exile, but Paradise. Exile comes if God goes away.

29 May – Life as prayer; work as liturgy; existence as return to God, with Mary as guide.

4 June – There are people threatening missiles and hurling insults, creating an atmosphere of war. This is the point we have reached fifteen years after the last catastrophe. It is the outpouring of atheism.

One might say that Christ has been crucified over again, in order to exclude him: loving humanity in the dreadful interval has only the Mother: his Mother became our Mother. To this unleashing of hatred, scorn and mechanical forces she opposes the sweetness which flowers from sacrifice: the sacrifice of not killing but letting her very Son, that Son, be killed for our redemption.

All that is left for us to do is to make ourselves in her, with her, under her, an *acies,* an army lined up for the struggle of love with hatred, of humility with pride.

6 June – Sometimes there springs up from the bottom of my soul a desire to see my studies and labours for the Church recompensed with praise and honours. What decadence it would be in my soul if I were to start cultivating such a vanity. One who has consecrated himself to God, through the Heart of Mary, cannot, possessing the love of the King, living in the house of the Queen, waste time hankering after praises of another type. Whoever possesses God possesses everything. And since a sort of curtain of silence has come down over my books and my name, it means that only the honour of the Church, the Mystical Body, now, justifies my work: it means that the Lord wishes to have me solely for himself. As for my writings, he does not know what to do with them: but he rejoices over my intentions. On the other hand, in the single audience which I had with the Holy Father John XXIII immediately after his election he compared me to a light shining high up on a candlestick, but which no one can see from close at hand. It is better like this.

24 August – I desired to imitate Mary at the germination stage of her sanctity: humility. And meanwhile, I cultivated criticism of the Church's actions, believing myself wise. This morning a simple soul shattered me by interpreting the actions I had criticised in a way which illuminated them: from a cave these were brought to a star. And this person put me on the ground *(humi)* in the sight of my nothingness: a nothingness which is filled up if it fills itself with God, a nothingness that deceives itself if it fills itself with the smoke of the self. And then

I promised to live in accordance with that wisdom which imposes upon me a ridiculous renunciation of my own judgement: and, I intend to observe, in the order given by wisdom, silence, unobtrusiveness, suffering and service: four words which I would like to deserve to have inscribed on my tomb, as supreme praise.

Often one reads in the newspapers of some aged person, usually an old-age pensioner, going up to the seventh floor and throwing himself down from there into the void, to put an end to his life: or more exactly, to put an end to the solitude from which he was suffering: the sickness of the old, people all at once transferred from the mass to isolation, from noise to silence.

It is a logical solution, even if mistaken, for it is indeed a question of going up to the top floor to hurl oneself from there into the abyss of God: into the chasm of immortal life.

The people who commit suicide have not understood the significance of that solitude, a significance which, besides, is not easy to understand.

Old age is a critical and decisive turning point: the stage of preparation for the meeting with the All, with the Eternal, with Beauty: the meeting with the warmth of youth which does not die. It is a period of evolution which is called involution: of progress which is called regression; of youthfulness in spirit, which is called senility.

Physical and moral discomfort denote trepidation at God's approach.

At that age, human life seems like a tree in winter. With the leaves fallen, the trunk opens its branches, naked and stiff, to heaven, and has no protection against rain, mist and lightning; but, free from the adornment of its leaves, it looks straight up, no longer deceived by foliage, no longer deceived by what suddenly flowers, grows and dies.

One grows accustomed to conversing with heaven, to probing the clouds, to explore the stars; and gradually one comes to notice a new world, not made up of noises and appearances. A discovery of the universe, which is usually covered up with ideological phantasms and printed paper, as well as the routine images of the day. Voices and lights of another world, bearing witness to the transcendental presence of a Father, a Creator, a Judge.

The old man who throws himself down into the courtyard is someone who, no longer warmed by human relationships, by the world's noise, by the vanities that are connected with money, has become frozen in his spirit and no longer has anything in view but the self: seen as an idol that is mocked, tormented and then forgotten; and seeing only that, throws himself into the void to reach it.

Catherine of Siena began the reform, the rebirth of old and young, celebrities and vagabonds, with the destruction of the self, an obstruction interposed between God and man. The self composed of vanity, is an encumbrance and a burden which demands suicide as an idolatrous act of worship to be rendered to the myth, the fable of one's own self.

In this way, two attitudes and two solutions confront one another; either destruction, the reduction of oneself to nothing, by throwing oneself from the seventh floor as a holocaust to death, or deification by emptying the person of all vanity to make it a hollow open to the divine and to be filled therefore with the life of God.

It is difficult to decide between the two.

Most people stop halfway, dangling between Life (God) and Death (Satan).

The man who cultivates the values of the soul often finds himself on the ridge of a crisis with a yawning chasm on either side, either of light or of darkness.

The mystics speak of the dark night. The christian, in the evening of his life, observes that he has worked for the Church and for the State and now he is laid aside, forgotten by ecclesiastical and civil authorities: he is not invited to meetings at which his competence was once appreciated; friends who were helped by him when they were boys and who have now become persons of consequence, pretend not to know him or treat him with condescension; sons, loved and served, now in possession of a career and a family of their own, forget him; institutions served with dedication and sacrifice, having found younger patrons, relegate him now to the fringe with elaborate hypocrisy.

It is a polar cold: from the pole of Death, where memory is extinguished. And it is possible that the reaction of discouragement and indignation may extend even to the church and to God, that injustice may be laid even at the Lord's door, for whose service one has laboured.

It is abandonment, solitude. At a certain moment, Jesus himself, who had bestowed bread and health, with an unending succession of miracles, on the unfortunate of every sort, had consoled and loved and served, to the point of restoring life to the dead, in his humanity felt the desolation of total abandonment when all the disciples had melted away and the crowd for whom he had done so much now insulted him and repaid their redemption with crucifixion. Then, in torment, he cried out: My God, My God, why have you forsaken me?

He was fully man and as such suffered the abandonment. But he solved the crisis in a salutary way, not by throwing himself down in despair but by committing himself into the hands of his Father: transferring his own anguish to God, who turned it into love and peace.

Love is the sap which makes the flower grow. In man, it feeds liberty; in love life reveals itself as a development into liberty: a process of liberation. We are so attached to our fetters that as they gradually fall away it seems to us a loss: and instead it is a gain. Glimpsing certain phases of this process my son S. said to me this morning: "Daddy, it rather looks as though your friends are casting you off . . ."

To banish such a thought from his mind and from mine, I replied, "It is a result of old age. When one is old, one is cast off: pensioned off, put on one side . . ."

But then, when I came to think it over more carefully, old age appeared to me as a stage of definitive liberation, with the final goal ever in view, the meeting between God and myself: God alone, I alone. As at the supreme judgment.

Here, on this feast of *Corpus Christi,* I am surrounded by the solitude of a prison. In spite of my awareness of the Mystical Body, the love of my family and the bond with my community, I feel myself alone: I am alone. He and I: God and I. To sustain this solitude, *Solus cum sola,* Alone with the alone, one would need a soul with the dimensions of love. But . . . if I were consecrated to Mary I would be a Marian sanctuary and I would contain a God; and I would meditate on one of the Blessed Virgin's virtues every day and possess fountains of love and my time would be full: I would not be alone. I would be with Mary. I would be Mary, and God therefore would be my fullness, my company.

But I still try to fill up the void with human affections, with the presence of creatures. And instead these exist more to be loved and comforted in their solitude than to bring me comfort. . . . Mary, if I possessed you, if I were in you, I would lack nothing. In fact, I do not lack anything. . . . And I look at the delicacy of Mary.

Immediately after these lamentations of mine she makes me read, in a foreign periodical, a thought of St. Thérèse of the Child Jesus. This virgin mother of ours said: "You dream of light, a fatherland of delights, you dream of the eternal possession of the Creator of these marvels, you believe that you will emerge one day from the darkness in which you are languishing. Go forward! . . . Go forward! . . . Rejoice over the death that he gives you, not that which you hope for, but a still deeper night, the night of nothingness!"

And the Imitation of Christ is quoted: "The man who is not ready to suffer all and to abandon himself entirely to the will of him whom he loves, does not know love."

Mary knew love and therefore Christ tested her to the point of repelling her: "Who are my Mother and my brothers?" . . . for to be his disciple one has to renounce oneself, take up the cross and follow her.

What joy, O Cause of our joy.

How many times I am mistaken in human affections: I give love and reap a harvest of grief. I plan an ascent and I come tumbling down; I think I am serving the Church and find myself blamed. . . . Then gulfs yawn before me, into which my ego leaps headlong, in desperation. . . .

But they are only moments: for, all at once, out of the silence there comes flying, as a kiss of the Holy Spirit, Our Lady, and gradually like a mother calling a child ever ready to break its neck, she restores my confidence and erects, along the slopes dampened by despair, the virginal and flower-covered walls of hope: and gradually she fills me with peace: and I see again the vanity of vanities, those of wealth and power, of fame and adulation. . . . She restores to me the upright and pure dignity of the sonship of God with the freedom which this involves, in regard to the powerful and the rich, friends that have failed me and friends that I have never had: a freedom that is as beautiful as Mary: which, indeed is Mary.

"O Jesus, I wish to be yours, yours as you intend: do with me all that you will." That is the formula of the morning consecration. and Jesus does what he wills: he wills me to be his, in his way: and he detaches me from all the ties of the world. He surrounds me with ever higher walls of silence: the aura of contemplation.

You would be a fool if you set yourself to contemplate yourself or your neighbour instead of fixing your soul on him and wresting from him charges of divinity: I have known men quite enough, I must know him very much better in this concluding phase of my existence, he who is life that does not die.

It is enough to weaken one's contact with God – prayer and contemplation in humility and charity – for the anguish of living to make itself felt. That weakening is in fact a substitution of the self for God: the self is a tyrant as exacting as it is cowardly: its spirit is fear, not love. To give oneself back to God is to bring into the game of one's life omnipotence, stability, joy: it is to separate from this state of considerations care for oneself, in order to be set free for caring only about one's brothers. Without God, what is life, what use is it? The young may still be enticed by the blandishments of illusion, that is by the prospect of some success: but for the old all that is left is reality: and reality is that only in God does one live. Outside him is non-Being, Satan, Death.

When you no longer find your own place in human relationships put yourself beneath all: and be in union with Mary: and you find God again, and God then puts you in your place, that which was determined by him from all eternity, *ab aeterno*.

When you cannot do any more and your last energies desert you, and you collapse, you still have one resource left: to collapse into the arms of God.

His Omnipotence is there also to sustain our power-lessness. Through it, what seems to be a fall on your part becomes a flight soaring upwards; it seems to be the end and it becomes a beginning.

For more than a month I have been ill, with an indis-position that causes me some little discomfort and, above all, keeps me housebound. I had not had any experience of illness, since my wound at the front. And therefore I have suffered from solitude and complained of it, experiencing the delusory character of my virtues of my repeated resolution never to complain. With my children to help me, I have realised what isolation and darkness I have tumbled into and at first I decided to react against it and regain a place amongst men. Then St. Teresa came to show me that this desolation is a miniature dark night, composed of regrets for the world: honours, fame, vanity. . . . And she made me see that it is a leap forward, towards union with God. *Solus cum sola*. He would have my soul for himself. And these detachments, rather than losses, are gains of further sectors of the freedom of the sons of God.

Holiness is an unceasing acquisition of freedom which costs blood. When God alone will live in me, what importance will the world's judgements and events in the world have, and what function will creatures exercise in regard to me save that of allowing me to love them in order to love, through them, Love?

Naturally in God there is no more solitude; there is plenitude; life, from the most arduous summit of which one sees the state in which so many of one's brothers are, laboriously seeking a reason for existence in materials and bonds of death.

1961

25 August – The meditations of these days are shifting my religious concern from its usual centre, which is man, to its legitimate centre, which is God. Previously, I used to contemplate my own wretchedness and that was my starting-point; now I contemplate the omnipotence of God and from there I go to what is human; which seen from the standpoint of the Creator, has value only to the extent that it remains within his plan and develops in accordance with his law. Outside of this, my self and all that is human is raw material for death: an approach to nothingness.

19 October – Consecrated to God. . . . Gradually the awareness of my condition as a consecrated person penetrates my being like a fermentation transforming all.

I understand our prayer ever better: "Christ's testament": "Consecrate them in the truth . . ." It is a self-immolation for truth, like Jesus Christ: a being on the Cross, a shedding of blood, a losing of all human joys . . . A being crucified, crucified together with Christ. By charity one puts oneself on the Cross, by truth one nails oneself to it.

And here is 'perfect joy'.

What gratitude I owe to the person who taught me that prayer, nailed me to that truth, crucified together with Christ!

2 November – This morning there were more people in church than usual and more communions. To communicate with the dead then, souls seek God, Life. And in a reciprocal way they avail themselves of the dead to communicate with God. They recognise thus that death is not a trauma between our life and the life of God, but a passage, a bridge: and since by cherishing the memory of the departed in prayer we feel ourselves nearer to the Eternal, death becomes a step forward towards Life.

"Blessed are the dead who die in the Lord." The Lord makes a beatitude of death.

1963

You want to stand on pedestals, shine, be seen; he hid himself in humanity, was born in a cave, died on a cross, shuts himself in tabernacles; the humblest, most hidden, least known dwelling-places, in silence, within ancient precincts.

30 April – Today is the feast of the Virgin of Siena (St. Catherine), of her who first set me on fire with the love of God.

I seem today finally to have made the move: the move of my being: from the self to God. During these last days, obstacles had multiplied to the extent that I seemed to have lost the decisive years of life. It seemed to me that, with the mistaken notion of following God, I had foolishly sacrificed a career: honours, art, society. . . . Now I feel that they were illusions, set alight in the dark by the Enemy. The choice is made. My frivolity is in the way, I know: but I trust for constancy and consistency in the Heart of Mary, in the help of St. Catherine, and, through them, in God himself.

The streets are ablaze and resounding with electoral manifestos, posters, broadcasts . . . the heart is drawn into the whirlpool of ambitions: and powerless, it suffers. . . .

When shall I decide to remove the centre of my life from the world to God, from agitation to peace, from the transient to the Eternal?

I delude myself sometimes that I have made my choice and anchored myself to life: but then I find myself again, by some tentacles, still bound to the changeable, to what is vain and perishable. . . .

And yet it is enough for me to fix my attention on him and put myself within the orbit of Mary's smile, it is enough for me to take myself out of myself and love others, for peace to be established in my spirit and for me to share in the security of the Eternal.

2 July – Solitude has come: and silence stretches over it like a feather mattress without edges, like this sea which gurgles as it laps the shore, coming from distant beaches over which a deep and clear sky extends its vault to protect the solitude.

Behind my shoulders is the land: but its noises are like

this murmuring of water, cradling my solitude. Men have withdrawn, friendships have faded; interests come to an end. . . . Ingratitude? Vanity? Illusions? To be sure! But it is above all the logic of existence which forces itself on a man up to a certain age; and then, the crest reached, the other side slopes downwards to plunge into mystery, like water in the depth of the sea.

Alone: therefore free.

Nature and supernature, in the service of an infinite intelligence, bring about this rest, and provide a stage of preparation for the Eternal; they snatch one from the uproar and the wear and tear of daily life to give some time for listening to silence: the voice of the Most High contained in the womb of mystery. The fickle prating of men has gradually withdrawn to a distance, leaving the soul to converse with those who are living the new life: the Life that does not die.

To regret the flattery of vanity, the hubbub of crowds, the itch for money, with all the mire of pride and scorn and calculations and hypocrisy, is like regretting the walls of a prison and its succession, hour by hour of work and hurried movements and meals and sleep, being afraid of oneself, of freedom, of being the judge of one's own steps and thoughts. *Deus nobis haec otia fecit.*★ But a god who is a God and leisure that becomes action for him.

Up to today I have worked more for man, for daily bread, now I work more for God, for our Father who is in heaven.

If the dominant tendency of this age, confronted with the lethal absurdity of division, is to re-establish dialogue with enemies and those far off, the dominant tendency of this age of repose, of the novitiate for Paradise, is to seek anew one's relationship with the Eternal and estab-

---

★ Virgil, First Eclogue: "A god has obtained this leisure for us" – spoken by Tityrus, alluding to the magnificence of Augustus.

lish the dialogue which does not betray nor entrap, but vivifies and exalts, the dialogue with God.

The world leaves us in order to leave us alone with God, in order that we may enter our fatherland: in a phase which is the preliminary formation for beatitude. Pedagogy for contemplation, after so much training for action.

Cast upon this unknown sea, fraught with silence as it is we repeat on another level the experience of Columbus, bearing Christ Christum ferens – Christopher, who, in the deserted ocean, halted alone, before a New World. With him it is well to prepare oneself and to pray: May Jesus and Mary be with us on our way, *Jesus cum Maria sit nobis in via*.

And then why do people say that the World is driving you out: or: the world is withdrawing from you?

But is it not rather that God is drawing near, giving you a hand to enable you to land on a quieter shore? He draws near and clears the countryside of all that litters the path: debris, and noise, smoke and branches which impedes your progress. If the world detaches itself at all, it is in the sense that contemplated in a certain way from above, by God, rather than from below, by the self, it reveals itself in its changeable vanity. One sees then that men withdraw from us to leave us in freedom, especially those to whom we had clung as to our ideal. With their sophistries and superficialities and at the same time with their sacrifices and heroisms, they appear as patterns of evil and of good, indications of the path to follow. And the lesson of news reports and accounts of current events is similar now that they are seen from a distance. . . .

For the silence in which the spirit takes its rest and relaxes after the cataract of fears that have been exploded over decades, freeing the judgement from complexes and prejudices and mythologies, makes it critically more agile in estimating the realities of the past and using them to give a direction to the future.

Seen in this simplicity, science is contemplated in its

ability to open new approaches to the mystery of the universe and to reveal beauties and daring ventures and immensities which inspire an ever increasing love, accompanied by adoration, of the Author of so many splendid things.

Struggles for justice and freedom are carried on in the context of generous efforts to save a superior heritage and to protect the glory of a lineage: while the champions of liberty and love, against backgrounds of darkness, offer new emphasis to these values, embraced by them with such energy precisely because they divinise, while hostility to them came from the Murderer, seeking to eradicate them. A profession, a career and every human relationship appear then as a dialectic of life and death; so that existence is seen to have been obstructed by haste and frenzy and distractions and has not been understood; it has not been lived: one has not had the time to understand it and live it and enjoy it: it has been like an arrow shot from the bow before one has had the chance to see it.

12 July – Social progress is the fruit of religious awareness, which makes us see in man our brother: indeed Christ himself. But religious awareness is favoured in its turn by social, cultural and political progress. If in the underdeveloped countries the average expectation of life is, in certain cases, thirty years, while in the developed countries it has risen above seventy years, the stage of rest, of silence in God, is facilitated and in many cases guaranteed by social institutions which are, in their turn, the flower and the fruit of the justice taught by the Gospel.

Religious awareness has not progressed in proportion to such a development; and too many people waste that period of quiet and recollection in regrets for the movement and the noise which appear to be the dynamism of life to those who live superficially.

Coexistence – so to speak – with God generates collaboration with him.

Existence in fact develops rationally if it becomes a collaboration with him who is God. This is an idea which, by itself, produces ecstasy: a God who treats us as collaborators, so that our activity, our words, writings, walls, laws, merchandise, art and science, technology and economics and politics are a participation in the work of building the edifice which the Creator untiringly constructs: a collaboration in bringing order into the universe, which, if it suffers from a disorder, suffers the loss of the freedom that was allowed us.

An ordinary but precious form of this co-operation is the provision of suffering: the sufferings which are lacking to no-one but belong especially to the final stage of life. They are united with the Passion of Christ Crucified to compose the material of redemption: a material which restores the balance of cosmic justice violated by freedom that has been mismanaged. And then, our attitude in regard to the Eternal is that of Christ on the Cross in regard to his Father, by whom he felt himself abandoned – and that was the peak of his suffering – anguish and yet abandonment to the will of the Most High, to the point of committing into his hands his own spirit.

This is the productive attitude. It costs atrocious sufferings, including the deepest solitude, in abandonment, if only for a moment, if only in appearance, by the Eternal, that is by Being.

But the outcome is a deeper insertion of our life into his, of our existence into his Being, so that it is born to newness of life precisely when it seems to be dying.

20 July – It is not true that men are abandoning you. Following the gravitation of the Eternal they are withdrawing in order to allow him to come, Alone, him, the Alone. And he wills to have the soul alone: *Solus cum sola*.

97

In this loving converse the youth of the Eternal began.

When I disregard my rule I cradle myself in the illusion that there is no harm in doing so: at my age, after the studies I have done, with my abilities, some trifle, a practice, a thought, does not seem capable of modifying the course of a soul. . . . But in fact that carelessness opens the door for the unobtrusive and silent entry of the Enemy, who, beneath the illusion of unconquered faith and solid virtue, undermines the very foundations of both.

In that confusion no more notice is taken of the collapse of God's work in us: rather, it seems that the demolition is an act of virtue: a diabolical illumination assists the havoc; exhibiting it as a mystical penetration: while it is a penetration, into emptiness.

You save yourself only by making of yourself nothing before God, obeying your Superiors, substituting his and their will for your own.

I had sunk to the lowest point of a psychic depression. Suddenly contact with my Superiors placed me once again on a light-filled platform. Truly, for a consecrated soul superiors are the path to Paradise: the link with God.

And I discovered that I had, indeed, given God my will but had kept back, like Ananias and Sapphira, some part of it. The words of my Superiors have enlightened me as to the beauty of losing all for the Lord, of sub-stituting his will for mine, so that, through the inter-mediary of those who are invested with authority, he may make of me what he wills. I say every morning:

"Jesus, I want to be yours; yours as you intend: do with me all that You want" (the words taught me by the person who directs me); but only now do I understand what they mean. They mean freedom: nothing which has to do with the world binds me any longer; God alone counts. I feel myself now truly consecrated: that is, belonging to him. And he can do what he wills.

If you have something against someone, even if the matter amounts to a true fault, you are wrong none-the-less to have it *against* him: love does not go against. And love *sees*. So that when you have something against, it is because you do not see; you do not see even that person's fault; for if you saw it you would weep and make it your business to eliminate it, loving the sinner, to set him free from his sin.

You have something *against* a person: therefore *against* Christ.

7 *August* – Living has become something artificial; an elaborate endeavour not to think about living, for life frightens. In its place are put drunkenness, narcotics, even work, even terror. A book has been published, awarded a prize into the bargain, which, without mincing matters, declares that there is nothing to be done, nothing to be believed, and reduces everything to killing time: a killing that has become an art, literature and science. In the end, the great ideologies are more elaborate ways of dazzling the crowds with myths. . . .

And instead life is too rich a complex of mysteries and of beauties, not to impose faith in an Author: and that vanity of false substitutes is too obvious not to lead to the only One who is true.

This, I know, contributes to isolating you: you abandon the game and they chase you away, they no longer see you: they look upon you as lost.

That is the reason for hermitages on the slopes of Everest or on Mount Athos, or on Monte Cassino: that is the reason for meditation and contemplation. But they presuppose a choice, a radical choice: for Life or for Death. The way of death is a turmoil of sounds, shouts, phantasms and trading in vanities, vice and alcohol. The way of Life is reality: the Way of the Cross, *Via Crucis*, but it leads to the resurrection, which is the definitive solution of the problem of our freedom.

Christ traversed it with his gaze fixed upon the Father, in the strength of love.

And the man who loves, sees God; he sees him already in every brother he loves. And the more he loves that brother the more he immerses himself in the contemplation of God.

This contemplation brings one close to God, enables one to reach the heights of Dante, of Catherine, of Teresa . . . that is, to see a vague and distant reflection of unbounded greatness. Man therefore approaches by degrees and contemplates by reflections.

The first object of contemplation for the man who thinks of God before the sea, under the sky, is the immensity of him, the Creator of these milliards of worlds, amidst which the earth is a tiny fragment. And yet for the inhabitants of the earth, God, from God, has become man. Truly to be everywhere in his creation, he becomes even little, tiny: he is Love and Love makes itself one with the loved person. He becomes a man amongst men, a morsel of bread for their food. To belong to other worlds, in his infinite inventiveness, He will have realised other marvellous forms of nearness and unity. Love has no boundaries.

The Infinite Spirit who becomes a human being is already to be seen in this emptying out of himself for Love. He becomes man in order that man may become God. In this way, the King draws near to his subject, the Creator to the creature, the Father to his son. Miracle of love, which brings the finite close to the infinite, and makes of us natural guests of this immensity.

An immensity which at times presents itself as an enormous bastion. The constellations, loaded with galaxies, involving distances that are counted in millions of light years, form a barrier which separates from the Author to such an extent that nothing of him can be discovered – or so it appears; while our soul is wrapped in an unfeeling coat woven of indifference and ignorance, so that the life of most people, or of the people who are best known, develops as if it had no purpose, no direction, no reason; and many kill themselves not having any motive for going on, or any tribunal before which to render an account. . . . With this in view St. Augustine said: "What else do I want to say, finally, Lord, but this, that I do not know from where I have come here, into this – I do not know what to call it – mortal life? or living death?"

And thus we are surrounded by a massive system of matter and of thought which removes God into boundless space.

And then in my inmost soul I feel the immensity of him who became man, who became bread: at a point so small as to seem inexistent: in the slightest of spaces.

I turn to the interior and listen to him: I live him: a conversation with the Eternal rather than with stars and planets is established in the depths of my being: and all the constellations and the worlds and the spaces appear as a tiny accessory extraneous to this reality: God in me; the Eternal in the mortal; the Good in the foolish. . . .

24 September – Sixty-nine years old: a point at which I have arrived without noticing it. I hoped for so many things from those years and the fruits gathered are other than those for which I hoped. It becomes clear that while I plundered, cut back, did harm, the divine Husbandman was correcting and giving life.

And he has brought me to the fruit of solitude: but as silence and pause for conversing with him, for being with him. Men have withdrawn into a distance for human motives; but at every withdrawal he was coming nearer. Now there are the two of us, he and I: the All and the nothing: Love and the Loved One. And the dialogue is not disturbed by the strident noise of friends and clients. . . . Then, if I go back amongst human beings, it is to love them, without presuming that I shall be loved in return, it is to serve them, without expecting to be served: not even by those who are closest in nature and in super-nature: so close and so distant! In such a way what seemed to be an abandonment by men has turned out to be a rediscovery of God – and in him are the Angels and the Saints, from Mary to the latest person to have died in a state of grace. It seemed to be a fall and it has been a lifting up to heaven. A liberation instead of a dispersion.

A sinister assault has been made upon me by the Enemy, confronting me with the balefully clear prospect of ingratitude and abandonment on the part of people I have loved and served. But I do not want the fact to depress or paralyse me: if I dwell upon it it grows like an atomic mushroom.

What is the ingratitude, the evil on the part of four, ten, a hundred human beings in comparison with the constant love of God, the ever grateful poetry of Mary, the protection of the saints and communion with them? Let the soul lose itself in the joy of love that has no sunset: that is not seen but felt; that does not make promises but upholds: let the soul lose itself in greatness rather than in wretchedness, in light rather than in shadows, in heaven rather than in earth.

My spiritual problems are solved if I examine them in the morning light, the transparent light of humanity. In it I see them with the clarity of Mary; and the thick shadows of pride, anger and vanity are dispelled like mist in the glad air of morning.

Every now and then it seems to me that the old man has finally died: but in fact, he dies three days after natural decease.

Thus one day the new man renounces pomps, friendships, vanities; the next day the old man rises from the tomb to shed tears over the loss of honours, privileges, friendships. . . .

And instead, if the pledge is worth anything which I took before Christ in the Blessed Sacrament on the feast

of the Immaculate Conception I am a man consecrated
to God, and that means that I no longer exist as a man of
the world. My will and my feelings are the will and the
feelings of my Superiors. If they set me on one side and
trample on me, it is for my good. I shall rise to God the
more I sink in the esteem of the world: to do the old
man to death means occupying the lowest place,
remaining hidden in silence. Obedience, penance,
humility: the three components of the life that has been
assigned to me by God.

1 November – One of the best of days: physical indis-
position has kept me at home, and at home I meditated
on Mary and my soul was filled with her: therefore with
poetry, beauty, purity. It was virginised.

And it is the feast of the Saints: they then reach their
culmination and are summed up in Mary, "Mother of
the Saints."

Being with her, I was in the Cenacle, which was
thronged with them.

1964

You contemplate yourself and you no longer see
anything. You see your brother and you contemplate
God.

"God has enclosed all in unbelief, in order to show
mercy to all." (St. Paul, Rom. 11. 32)

Nonetheless, humility to the point of making yourself nothing is not to be understood as abjection or
degradation. It is the state of receptivity to love in the
dignity and the freedom of the sons of God. The humble
soul is filled with the Holy Spirit; the base soul is filled
with self-love, reduced to refuse. It does not serve for
God's sake; it serves for its own sake. It does not love
and therefore does not give itself to others;it loves itself

and therefore serves to obtain, to reduce to nothing; it serves itself.

Humility is the most sublime virtue: indeed the foundation of dignity. A Virgin Mary who would behave in a servile fashion, ready to seek praise, that is falsehood, is inconceivable. And on the other hand, cowardice is the basest of passions, paying to its own self a worship conducted with materials taken from the dustbin.

And therefore: humility, like Mary, without flattery or weakness is far removed from abjection.

Usually vice is a form, more than anything else, of stupidity. For the man who adulates, pays court, demeans himself to obtain favours, ends up by causing disgust: he produces nausea: and so he repels and keeps at a distance where he seeks to attract and bring near.

Serve your neighbour, your Superiors, but with dignity and detachment: then it is charity, otherwise it is sordidness. St.Francis of Sales gives the rule: "Ask for nothing, refuse nothing". Serve, but not in order to serve yourself.

12 July – During these months the dialogue has become more intense, more intimate, as gradually so many remnants of vanity have fallen all round me like dry leaves. A complete reversal has taken place in my spirit, as a result of which it seems to me at times that, while a year ago I yearned after God from the earth, now I have the impression of looking at the earth from God: and that means that there has been a transposition, even if with relapses. Human sentiments have been purified by contact with the divine: I do not love the persons who are dear to me any the less: I love them in God; so that I no longer suffer from their being far away, since a unity has been achieved which is beyond space and time. Nature no longer surrounds me like a springboard from which to soar to the heights; but I contemplate it from on high as the resplendent masterpiece of the Eternal.

My enthusiasm for work has been considerably reduced, amongst other reasons because physical strength has decreased: but in its place there has entered a relaxed and luminous quiet which resembles this clear sky, extending its vault over the sea that stretches away without limit.

The spirit of the Council and Pope Paul VI's *Ecclesiam Suam* have increased my soul's social and priestly awareness. My soul is glad and ready to insert the sacred into every action of the day as if it had discovered a new dimension to existence and the secret for piercing at every point and at every moment the barrier of shadows interposed between God and man, between heaven and earth, between the eternal and the contingent.

Thus from day to day life grows. It is no longer a merely biochemical process interspersed with speeches and illusions, with poetry and noises. No: it is also and above all a penetration of the divine into us and an insertion of ourselves into the design of the Creator, into the will of the Judge, into the love of his essence. The things of the world are means, and they fashion the passage: they are not life, they serve it – even evil, even enmity, even the death of persons who are dear to us. Now Eletto Folonari has died (12 July 1964): but for one who lived with him and knew his soul, that death is seen as an offering, a sacrifice, made on behalf of the religious work to which he was dedicated: and in the light of the Eternal God, in which he lived, his tragic demise appears as the picking of a magnificent flower by God, who was in love with it: a preference of his love which will have caused Eletto to be welcomed upon his entry into Paradise by the saints and the angels exclaiming: "At last he's ours," gathered around Mary who will have been holding by the hand his father, now his brother for all eternity.

And this life of the spirit, diffused through all heaven and earth, without any break in its continuity, since in every place if God is there, Paradise is there, may be denied on the pretext that the surgeon does not encounter it beneath his scalpel nor the astronaut in the course of his flight, but what is spirit is perceived by the spirit, a sixth sense which sees and welcomes the wonders of the Eternal in time. What do we know of the human organs for apprehending the divine if it was only yesterday that radar, radiogrammes, wireless telegraphy, TV, etc. were invented? Some men have penetrated further into the mystery of God: the Prophets, Mary, Paul, Dante, Teresa, Augustine and Francis. . . . But all men, if they succeed in freeing themselves from all those material things which isolate a man, succeed in communicating with eternal Life and bring back from it nourishment for temporal life. He who seeks finds.

Silence no longer causes dread: it is sought, in order that the Eternal may dwell in it and breathe forth the Word in it. The desolation of past years no longer has any meaning: I wanted the company of men and they fled from me; now the void is filled with God and God is a companion who does not leave one alone, does not allow one to remain lost. His voice fills the worlds, fills the soul. . . . What an illusion to have substituted for it the noise of records, tittle-tattle, motors, trafficking. . . .

The secret is to create silence, be it only within the spirit, to listen to the Word, as Mary did. I no longer have any desire to write or speak: I long to hear that voice, which penetrates the worlds.

21 August – This mystery becomes ever clearer and ever simpler, as gradually the soul is clarified and reduces things to the Absolute. God alone: to place ourselves in him; we see the rest being given back but it is transformed. Everything settles into its hierarchic place, if only it is considered from the peace of this divine atmosphere.

God is not complicated, he is simple. There is no need of difficulties in order to reach him: what is needed is simplicity. That is why working-class women, girls and

106

ardent young men find him at once, directly, sometimes more quickly than theologians who know the complex stages of the ascent to God.

Knowledge helps, but it is not enough. Love is needed. And then one can converse with God or more exactly, listen to God, in the depths of the Spirit, even in the midst of occupations: the silence of Paradise, wide open in us, banishes noise.

If we wait for science to discover transcendence, we shall have to wait perhaps for some millions of years. Today, we discover that primitive man dates from two million years before our era. It has taken science two million years to discover the content of the atom; it has still not discovered the cancer virus. This is because the way to God does not pass through the laboratories where scientific research is conducted, even if these can always furnish aids: and they do furnish them.

This conversion appears therefore only as a change of route: it is also a return from dispersion to the true way: that which goes from God to God, traversing the waste-land of trial. Now I feel that I am flying, from moment to moment, towards him, inaccessible and yet close at hand. So near that already I am beginning to be in him. Previously union seemed to me a being *with* God: now, it appears to me a unity, which is a being *in* God to the point of becoming him. That is understandable to the extent that the soul, daughter of God, can unite itself with its Father. And yet, even a drop in an Ocean is ocean; even a soul, an infinitesimally small atom, if lost in God, is God by participation.

And the relationship winds through all the degrees of the divine economy.

We are one with Mary, one with the angels and the saints.

The same unity is established with the Church. In regard to her I am no longer in an attitude of service while at the same time being independent and often in an attitude of criticism. Now, I am in the Church: her law is my law, her trial my trials.

Now I am in God: I am God by participation: and he is freedom, love and repose.

Substitute God for the self; the new man for the old: this is a vast gain, and very evidently such.

Its consequences, logically, are felt even in human society, in civil, political and economic relations. . . . To give an example: never as now have I been united with my wife, the image, as never before, of the Church: united in a relationship which has become sacred, in which I feel that the nuptial union of Christ with the Church is beginning to be realised.

Always there, by supernatural gravitation, one falls back on love. And to love is to become the other. *The other*, who in the world may be the one who is different, the enemy, ceases to be such, for the two become one.

Making yourself one, which absorbs the will, the feelings and thought, and nonetheless does not absorb the person: in fact it establishes a dialogue. A dialogue which generates familiarity.

Such is prayer, the effect of which is that you feel that you belong to the family of God in heaven and to the household of Nazareth on earth, where Mary is really your mother, the most beautiful and the purest and the greatest of mothers.

However it is certain that this consecration of oneself to God, to the point that one can say: it is no longer I who exist, what exists is an instrument of God's will, seems like making yourself nothing to those who worship gladiatorial poses. And it is so; but in a sense opposite to theirs. The self is supplanted by God: and God gives the person a participation in the divine nature, which means strength, freedom and an end to fear.

The man consecrated to God is one who has had the courage to effect the greatest revolution: that which frees him from the servitude of avarice, lust and vanity: it tears him away from conformity and saves him from standardisation.

No longer afraid, upheld by the Eternal, he enters into Mary's marshalled host, which confronts evil, personified in Lucifer. And he is in that army not to take his leisure but to make effective his pledge to fight in the Church militant. Catherine of Siena and Joan of Arc were two mystics: but from contemplation they derived the driving force for action.

Thus the obligation to love one's brothers, that is to serve them, which derives from that consecration, appears to be a curtailment, because it leads the person who loves to take up a rear position in the ranks and, as far as level is concerned, to place himself underneath: to make himself a servant. In the paradox of the Christian revolution freedom is freedom to love and love means serving: therefore it is freedom to become servants. But it is a voluntary service, rendered in full liberty: therefore a maximum exercise of free will. Who could be freer than Vincent de Paul, the servant of the poor, than Peter Nolasco, servant of slaves, who sold himself as a slave? Who could be freer than the Marchesa Maddalena di Canossa, who devoted herself to solacing the misery of the San Zeno quarter in Verona, coming as she did from a palace which had entertained Napoleon and the Hapsburgs?

Jesus, free as only an omnipotent God can be free, emptied himself: made himself nothing to become the universal servant.

The opposite attitude replaces freedom by arrogance, and makes power consist in reducing to the status of servants as many as possible of one's brothers, free sons of God. Against love tyranny sets itself up. Either God or a master. Either love or servitude, that veritable servitude which crushes the person.

26 August – I have delivered so many speeches. . . . But there was no need for them, it seems to me. In the end, it is a question of a simple technique. You mount to God to the extent that you descend amongst men: the steps are mortification, penance, obedience, humility, making yourself nothing.

These truths are repeated in all the books on asceticism. But to drive them into the head of a layman, and a layman who for decades has attached overwhelming importance to fame, pride and vanity, a catapult of exceptional dimensions is needed.

I have kept him at a distance also by the mistaken desire of gaining him by exceptional ways. Satan asked Christ to throw himself down from the pinnacle of the Temple in order that the angels might come and bear him up on their wings. . . . The man who makes himself into an angel, becomes a devil, said St. Teresa, or words to that effect.

Man goes to God as a man: the angel goes to God as an angel. To add the divine to the human is something holy: to take the human element away from humanity in order to facilitate the ascent to the divinity is inhuman and the inhuman is a descent towards the Satanic.

Do not look then for levitations and visions: these are gifts which God gives to whom he wills. Expect to live the divine as a man and so to draw near to the Man-God, who, to come to meet us, lived the human as God, that is, in accordance with his nature. It is in this way that the meeting between Christ, Man–God, and man deified after the pattern of Mary comes about. She never attempted to escape from the limits of her own nature: she was a virgin, a betrothed maiden, a married woman, a mother, a widow, with all the burdens and obligations of her state in the world. Thus she mounted to God, because she assimilated her own human will to the divine will in such a way as to make a unity of them.

The secret of holiness can be summed up like this. And since it is the will of a God who is Love, this assimilation consists in loving.

It is all easy, even if difficult to carry into effect: and it

110

is all simple, without any intrusion of magic or phantasy.

In love one understands the path by which the reascent to God is made, for love is ascribed appropriately to the Holy Spirit, and he was the spouse of Mary.

Truly, in God there are neither servants nor masters, neither men nor women: and Mary can be copied, to the extent that that is possible, also by men. She belongs to all, she has served and does serve both men and women.

And she is the Virgin, Mother of Christ.

Even a married man, burdened with years and faults, can, by his conversion, make his spirit virginal: and he does it with the oxyhydrogen flame of love: that is, by uniting himself with the Holy Spirit, Spirit of love.

Then the soul, united to God as to its spouse, to the Spirit of God, can give Christ to society, bringing the Church, the Mystical Christ, to birth.

And in this operation one is associated with the life of the Blessed Trinity, and attains to the highest level.

To humble oneself, to hide oneself, to disappear like Mary, amounts to seeking the most favourable conditions for establishing a dialogue with God. Life hitherto has been a dialogue, or at worse, a wrangle, with man.

Now life begins again through communication with God; and in that communion one understands man and has compassion for him.

In this understanding a spirituality, a direct relationship with God, or a charity, a relationship with God through men, which seeks gifts, prizes, gratitude or affection, no longer has any meaning. . . . Charity does not lead to human endearments, but to inhuman solitude. At the centre of your good deeds, your quest for holiness, you find yourself at a certain moment like Christ in the Garden: the people on whom you have conferred benefits are far away and asleep, the disciples themselves under the trees are sleeping. You are alone, and if you make yourself more holy you will be on the Cross, where the people on whom you have conferred benefits will yell their derision at you. One does good for God not for man: for love of the Creator, not to have the love of creatures. In this way you are an aerial, bringing the divine into the human.

12 October – My present feeling of freedom in regard to the world and to men is most remarkable. Now I love man, but in God, as God loves him: that is, I must love man not for myself, for my good, but for his good in God, for God. God is not loved if man is not loved: man, who is a sacrament of God for us. Without my brother God does not come to me, normally. But who robs me of my freedom to love man? No one. Except that such freedom involves also being free from man: I will serve him, yes, but enslave myself to him, no. God alone is necessary.

The modern saint is often not connected with a religious community: he does not shut himself up, but goes out and about in the world, has contacts with men. Yet, if he loves them in God, if in everything he does the Will of God, if love purifies his soul from moment to moment, he becomes virginal.

For the married layman his consecration is something different. He is linked with God, he is an instrument of God; he lives God. And, religiously, he is bound by a bond which constitutes and is the equivalent of an enclosure, that is, obedience. By it, even in the tram, in his office, in a cafe, he is attached to the rule, to his Superior, and, by it, to God: by obedience, he is always in the orbit of the sacred.

1965

You know how to live; and you do not live in accordance with that knowledge.

You live if it is not you who live but Christ who lives

112

in you. And Christ takes up his abode in you if your self moves out: this pompous idol, made of clay, which affords the Adversary a lodging.

You know this: and then why, to defend yourself from supposed downgrading, from offences, humiliations, misunderstandings (and so forth) do you judge your Superiors, that is, those who represent for you the thought of God and the will of God?

All your torment is here: the waste of time, and your uneasiness, which touches on despair. Ah, half-wit!

21 June – The trunk of this tree is becoming ever more naked. With the flowers gone and the fruit picked (who has eaten it?) the leaves have fallen and the branches are all broken. Humanly speaking it would be a matter for despair: from on high the world offers the spectacle of rampant violence, narcissism, ambition, the worship of money, envy. It would be a matter for despair, as in fact so many old-age pensioners do despair, throwing themselves out of fifth-floor windows. Divinely on the other hand there are grounds for hope: for that reduction is a reduction of man in order that God may grow: there is always the compensation, almost the union of divine and human nature, but the part of God grows, endeavouring to become all, until the day comes when you will not be there any longer; he is there and you become part of him: and from nothing you become everything.

22 June – My intellectual powers are still vigorous, as is plain to see from my speeches, writings etc. Why, I was thinking again this morning, have I been deprived of political, journalistic and literary activity? Because God was reserving this part of my life for himself: his will for me is not politics, journalism or literature, but holiness.

It is a clearly manifested will and I am resolved to carry it out at all costs.

21 October: St. Ursula – My mother's name has brought me nearer to the heavenly Mother and through her to Jesus. The greater this closeness becomes, the greater the light showing up the realities which seek to hide beneath the darkness of self-idolatry, this offering of incense to one's own self.

Thus I see again for the hundredth time that reality lies on the level of humility, that is, in being the servant of one's brothers.

It is a radiant vision, bringing peace and joy.

Pride on the other hand darkens and gives rise to resentment exteriorly, discouragement interiorly: and in that darkness relations with others are no longer understood. One's Superior, who should be the image of God, becomes a masked despot and instead of the joy of obedience there is worry and the desire to sever one's connection and so to tumble into nothingness: a land of thistles and of pits amidst brambles.

1966

When you will have no concern other than the glory of God, when you will open the eyes of the soul and see nothing but God in heaven and souls on earth, when you will no longer see yourself in any moment, then you will be free: you will no longer belong to that gathering of ambitions, passions and greed which form your self – Nothingness – but you will belong to Life, to Eternity, to God, who is All.

1968

It is, I believe, the 4th of January.

I am a victim of the influenza epidemic which has laid my wife low also: a temperature of 102.

I am reading about theology without God, the Death of God. . . . Sheer boredom. . . . One signpost remaining

114

amidst the breakdown: art leading to God, reason leading to God . . . to Life.

What a bore these conceited champions of Death are! They want to take God away from us in order to reduce us to the despair to which the Murderer tends: the non-existence of man and the absurdity of life. It is indeed wonderful what man's imagination can accomplish when it sets itself to conjure up lugubrious wraiths who extinguish life. Fortunately you are there, Mary: you who rise, rise again after every collapse into imbecility on our part.

But this means that the hour has come, the final hour for you, for starting to live in accordance with the will of the Author of Life:

(1) Give love, however much indifference, pride, imbecility you may encounter: despairing and oversubtle pretexts for aloofness.

(2) Unite yourself with God, as Love, wholly, without any further reservations, double-talk or half-measures.

(3) Be a living image, a witness, of the living Church, Love inserted into a technological, economic and bureaucratic world.

Existence, if you know how to interpret it and give it its full value, is an ascent to the divine: a continual abandoning of human beings in order to leave yourself alone with God: *solus cum sola*.

We complain of betrayals or desertions, cloaked in specious reasoning, when in fact they are only the preparation for this meeting with God – for the moment at which, your obsession with earthly cares has finally ended – you can converse, in the Father, in the Creator, with the Eternal and Infinite, refuse of mere nothingness as you are.

6 April – Passion week. Tomorrow is Palm Sunday. Events continue more than ever to rob me of all that can attract in existence: they are pushes directing me towards the Cross. From on high he attracts us and it is time for me to accept with joy this sharing in his death in order to share in his redemption. What is happening lays bare my wretchedness, my littleness: but this justifies the Cross where, alone humanly, I am with Christ divinely.

To live is to open oneself; to die is to shut oneself up. If the seed does not die, that is, if it does not develop and flower and bear fruit, it dies. And man dies because he spends his time in cultivating himself; he shuts himself up in himself: and he suffocates, amidst torments. He lives if he expands with love, and thinks no longer of himself but of his neighbour, seen as the representation of God; and in God, who is life, he too lives.

All the anguish (the agony) of this locking up of myself in myself, when outside there is the universe: God, beauty, joy, life.

7 *May* – The Lord has taught me a lesson, in which love and severity are blended. I thought I had made some few steps forward if only modest ones, and that I had gained a certain security. And instead I have succumbed to anger, wretchedly. If I had made a step forward, it means that progress in holiness is a progress in risk too: as virtue grows, temptation grows. There are grounds for maintaining that while the Saints are watched over by God, the Adversary controls them also, who drops on them with an opposing power in proportion to the virtue that has been acquired.

The moral: without God's help we are nothing.

1 *December* – If a person does not wish to believe, he is free not to believe. God has impressed the seal of his greatness on man by making him free. Only he teaches man to use freedom as freedom from evil and not freedom from good. In God man is free to love: that is, to live; against God, he is free to do evil, that is to die.

He who seeks finds. He who seeks God, finds him.

He who listens for him, hears him. His voice teaches us continually to reverse current opinions in order to bring men and things firmly into the divine plan, which is immortality in beauty.

Illness torments: the man who accepts it in the spirit of Christ Crucified makes of it a chemical process of self-purification and a contribution to the Passion of Christ. A certain man is ungrateful, odious: looking at him again with the eyes of our common Father, he becomes my brother, who needs my help. Certain words offend us: if we examine them in the light of God the Father, they afford us an opportunity for suffering and forgiveness, that is, for making a leap forward in the ascent which ordinarily perhaps would take years of reflection.

The Lord shows the other face of things: the face which he sees them from. Evil is turned into good, suffering into love, human solitude into a conversation with the angels and the blessed, with Mary and with the Trinity. Prison is transformed into freedom, in the fields of Paradise; hunger into a holocaust to God. Poverty becomes wealth, disgrace becomes glory; darkness is full of light.

We notice that evil men who seemed to oppress us become our collaborators; involuntary agents of our holiness. Ugliness thus becomes beauty, misfortune an opening to grace. History grinds like a noisy and dusty mill, from which flour issues; and from it bread is made. It is an engine which, with earthly materials, war, struggles, epidemics, hatreds and also with grain, water, metals and terrestrial energies, prepares for an approach to the spirit. And the whole of creation is seen, as it appeared to St. Paul, to yearn to converge on Christ, where the definitive grafting of human and divine, of earth and heaven, of matter and spirit, takes place.

The man who looks only at the earthly, fleeting, negative aspect, seen from this world, looking towards the human sphere, renounces the more extensive region

117

of life: he becomes only an object of death, of which men and events make themselves the authors.

Christmas is drawing near. For a man who sees with only one eye what is approaching is cold, darkness and hunger. For the man who sees things in God, with both the human and the divine eye, the Redemption is approaching, which is joy, life and deification.

Christmas, an image of the paradox that the Redemption constitutes for men. It reveals the ways in which the heavenly Father acts, who makes of a stable the abode of the Eternal, the meeting-place of purity and beauty. He can make the God-Man come to birth in the bare and tattered dwelling of an old man, a person who is the temple of the Holy Spirit, if he wishes, and so a meeting-place for angels singing to the universe.